AF689531

Angang Hu
Guangyu Hu

Achievement Evaluation of IFI Assistance Loans to China (1981—2002)

Angang Hu
Guangyu Hu

Achievement Evaluation of IFI Assistance Loans to China (1981—2002)

With 30 figures

TSINGHUA UNIVERSITY PRESS

Springer

EDITORS:

Prof. Angang Hu,
Center for China Studies, School of Public Policy & Management,
Tsinghua University,
100084, China
E-mail:anganghu@tsinghua.edu.cn

Dr. Guangyu Hu,
Center for China Studies, School of Public Policy & Management,
Tsinghua University,
100084, China
E-mail:hugy@tsinghua.edu.cn

ISBN 978-7-302-14132-7 **Tsinghua University Press, Beijing**
ISBN 978-3-540-45888-3 **Springer Berlin Heidelberg New York**

Library of Congress Control Number: 2006940058
This work is subject to copyright. All rights are reserved, whether the whole or part of the material is concerned, specifically the rights of translation, reprinting, reuse of illustrations, recitation, broadcasting, reproduction on microfilm or in any other way, and storage in data banks. Duplication of this publication or parts thereof is permitted only under the provisions of the German Copyright Law of September 9, 1965, in its current version, and permission for use must always be obtained from Springer-Verlag. Violations are liable to prosecution under the German Copyright Law.

© 2007 Tsinghua University Press, Beijing and Springer-Verlag GmbH Berlin Heidelberg
Co-published by Tsinghua University Press, Beijing and Springer-Verlag GmbH Berlin Heidelberg

Springer is a part of Springer Science+Business Media
springer.com

The use of general descriptive names, registered names, trademarks, etc. in this publication does not imply, even in the absence of a specific statement, that such names are exempt from the relevant protective laws and regulations and therefore free for general use.

Cover design: Frido Steinen-Broo, EStudio Calamar, Spain
Printed on acid-free paper

Executive Summary

Abstract

On April 17 and May 15, 1980, the International Monetary Fund (IMF) and the Board of Executive Directors of the World Bank adopted a resolution, deciding to accept the People's Republic of China as representative of "China" and restored the legal seat of the People's Republic of China in IMF and the World Bank.

World Bank is the largest global development aid agency and also a foreign organization that has lent the largest amount of money to China. From 1981, when the World Bank provided the first loan for funding China's university development, to the end of 2000, it provided China with a total of nearly US$34.2 billion loans for 259 projects. Of these projects, 157 have been completed, 102 are still in progress and 15 others are in the preparation stage. China has become the No. 1 borrower from the World Bank in the world.

The Asian Development Bank (ADB) is a regional development aid agency in Asia. China became a full member in 1986. The amount of loans ADB provided for China is only next to that by the World Bank. By the end of 2000, it had provided China with a total of US$10.181 billion loans for 80 projects. Before 1990s, the total ADB loans to China were US$460 million. Most of the ADB loan projects were performed after 1990s.

Background

This is the first comprehensive study conducted by Center for China Study at the request of the International Department, Ministry of Finance, to evaluate the overall performances international assistance and to analyze lessons learnt over the past 20 years. On the one hand, the study analyzed various effectiveness and contributions of the international assistance to the Chinese economy from a macro point of view. On the other hand, the study investigated, on a micro basis, the actual implementation of the projects and their financial, economical, social, ecological, knowledge and system innovation efficacy. The study drew the successful experience in the cooperation between the Chinese government and international financial institutions (IFIs), analyzed major problems existing and lessons learnt in project management and provided recommendations on how to further develop international cooperation that is mutually beneficial. It took us one year to conduct large amount of investigation, information collection, calculation and analysis. IFI strategy and planning reports, as well as their evaluation reports, were referred to during our investigation. Ministry of Finance had invited relevant domestic experts for discussion and solicited comments and suggestions to this report.

Overall Evaluation

In 1978, China is a closed economy with neither internal nor external debt. Although the population in China accounted for 22% of the world population, the total export was less than 1% of the total world exports. At that time, China was one of the poorest countries in the world; per capita GDP was only half of the average level of low income countries. China had neither financial resources nor economic reform experience for economic construction. The development level in agriculture, energy and transportation sectors are very low. Enterprises suffered from out-of-date technology and management, insufficient technical professionals and skilled workers. Hundreds of millions of people lived in poverty with nearly one-third of the population illiterate or half illiterate. China was at the beginning of an economic development encountered the situation of underdevelopment and property and after the third session of the Eleventh National Congress of the Communist Party of China, which was a very important beginning to China's opening to the outside world, the Central government decided to join the World Bank and make use of loans of IFIs. Gradually, the world has started to know China and China has integrated into the world.

Over the past two decades, China has become one of the largest recipients of IFI loans. The total loans received accumulated to RMB417.6 billion yuan and total project funding amounted to RMB1,000 billion yuan. The international financial insititutions (IFIs) have provided highly effective assistance for various key sectors in China that were designed to promote Chinese economic development through active international cooperation and achieve mutual benefits and win-win for all parties. On the one hand, the international assistance served as a propeller in the reform, opening to the outside world and development in China. On the other hand, the development miracle of China made four major contributions to the global development, namely contribution to growth, contribution to trade, contribution to poverty reduction and contribution to development. The relationship between IFIs and China is not a simple relationship of lender and borrower, but a new successful relationship of "cooperation, mutual beneficiary and win-win for all parties".

Our study shows that among almost all the lower income countries, the percentage of IFI loans in total domestic investment and per capita loan received in China are the lowest. However, the macro economic performance indicators are very high in China. The project success rate is high and the performance of IFI loans is the best. Similar conclusions can be found in the Operation Evaluation Reports of the World Bank and the Asian Development Bank. Mr. Li Lanqing, Former Deputy Prime Minister spoke highly of the IFIs and their assistance: "The World Bank and other foreign government favorable loans have played very positive roles in our education, human resources development, basic infrastructure construction and enterprise technology renovation."[1] The evaluation of the Evaluation Department of the World Bank concluded that the project performance in China is above the world average, the satisfactory levels of many of the projects are way above the world average. According to the Asian Development Bank's evaluation, China is one of the best countries in ADB projects implementation. China's project performance is consistently better than the overall level. All these reflected that Chinese government had very strong project management and implementation capability and very good internal control system [2].

One of the most important significances of receiving loan assistance from IFIs for China is that it helped China smoothly open its closed economy to the outside world, end China's long-standing isolationism and integrate China with the rest of the world. Mr. Deng Xiaoping has repeatedly emphasized that "opening to the outside world has profound significance. Any nation that tries to develop will not achieve its goal if it isolates itself from the rest of the world. It is impossible for a country to develop if it does not increase international exchange, learn from advanced experience and technologies and make use of capital from developed countries"[3]. IFI loans brought with them development knowledge, innovative technologies and management experience that made Deng Xiaoping's idea conceivable and realistic.

The roles of IFI loans can be described as follows.

1. Role of seed money. During 1980s, international assistance provided timely assistance badly needed in China and helped China broke the bottleneck. Since 1990s, China's reform has entered a period of tackling the difficulties. IFIs played a role of knowledge bank by providing more development knowledge and technical assistance.

2. Role of demonstration. Since the development projects conformed to China's development strategy, they are both very feasible and repeatable. They had played a very good demonstrative and promotional role.

3. Role of catalyst. The IFI loans directly promoted the regional development of the recipient areas and people, such as provided necessary infrastructure,

improved basic living condition and created better investment climate. The technical assistance and policy advisory services played a very important role in disseminating knowledge and more effectively promoted the overall reform and development in China.

In addition, the loans from IFIs made substantial contributions to promoting development in China in following six areas.

1. Development viewpoint contribution. This is the greatest contribution of international development assistance. The development viewpoint developed by international organizations, such as Sustainable Development, Comprehensive Development (World Bank, 1999), Millennium Development Goals (United Nations, 2000) and Respect Human Dignity (United Nations, World Bank, etc. 2002), had profoundly influenced and promoted China's new development viewpoint of putting people first and "five balanced aspects" strategy (raised at the third session of the Sixteenth National Congress of the Communist Party of China). During different time period, the World Bank and the Asian Development Bank (ADB) have developed assistance strategies and plans respectively to conform to Chinese government's strategy and assisted China, the country with the largest population, to achieve "Millennium Development Goals" ahead of schedule.

2. Investment contribution. The IFI loans have directly bridged the funding gap of the Chinese government during 1980s, which was very large in comparison to the domestic budget at that time. Indirectly, IFI loans induced more foreign direct investment (FDI), domestic private investment and total investment by improving investment climate through improving basic infrastructure and public services. According to our calculation, the IFI loans increase by US$1, the FDI would increase by US$1, and domestic private investment would increase by over US$3. Currently, China has become the biggest developing country with the largest private investment and FDI in-flow.

3. Infrastructure contribution. IFI projects dramatically improved transportation, city construction, energy, water treatment and wastewater treatment in China. The World Bank and ADB had played a very important role in promoting the development of railway and highway construction. The projects not only adopted advanced technologies, but also introduced incentive system such as charging user fees. Within just two decades, China has quickly become the country with the second longest highway system in the world.

4. Poverty reduction contribution. Poverty reduction is one of the key areas in international development assistance since 1990s and one of the most effective assistance. The poverty reduced or estimated population in China during the past two decades is the largest in the world.

5. Knowledge and system development contribution. Another important role that the World Bank and ADB played is that their high quality experts took advantage of extensive international experience, global knowledge network and policy advisory research and study reports to provide knowledge and experience

for China's development. To China, they are more of a provider and spreader of global development knowledge and experience than creditors and providers of international capitals. In order to support China's economic transition, the World Bank and the ADB have made recommendations on system building that covered many sectors, such as state-owned enterprises reform, social security system reform, government restructuring, financial and fiscal system reform. In the meantime, China became one of the most successful models of transitional economies and became an important source for development experience.

6. Sustainable development contributions. The green assistance strategy of preserving ecological environment and preventing pollution adopted by IFIs supported China's transition from traditional resource intensive growth model with high pollution emissions to a new green growth model of environmental protection and energy saving.

IFI Loan Projects Implementation Evaluation

IFI projects cover almost all the economic sectors in China and had made significant contribution to the economic development in every part of China. The outcome of the study shows that the performance of IFI projects is very successful both from macro and micro points of view. In the nine sectors that IFI loans operate, seven are rated as successful, which accounted for 78% of the total operation.

First of all, the overall project operations are pretty successful. Most of the projects have met the targets set during the project preparation and the implementations are satisfactory, especially agriculture, energy and health sector projects. For eastern regions, IFI loans expanded financing channels for private enterprises through improved investment climate and operation environment, promoted the inflow of FDI and strengthened the integration with domestic and foreign markets. For central and western regions, IFI loans promoted inflow of capital through improving local infrastructure and changing development viewpoint, thus promoted the economic growth of the less developed regions.

Second, during the project implementation, project implementation entities emphasized on introducing foreign project management experiences, system innovation and system building, thus resulting in positive externalities and demonstrative effects. They have accumulated rich experiences and lessons for the same kind of projects in project preparation, management, implementation and post evaluation. In fact, IFI project management, innovation in management system and establishment of coordination mechanism for various levels of management agencies have all became the models for project operation of similar projects within the same sector.

Third, from the impact evaluation point of view, IFI loans had very positive macro effects and played significant roles in social, economical and environmental development, as well as public services and public finance construction. Most IFI projects are for the benefits of the public, which provided large volume of public goods. Among them, the implementation of basic infrastructure projects have greatly improved infrastructure, the business operation and investment climates of all the regions, especially the central and western regions that lagged far behind in economic development. They have significantly promoted the economic development of the less developed regions, increased the local per capita income, improved people's standard of living. Health and education projects reflected the development viewpoint of putting people first and protected the interest of the disadvantaged groups. They improved the quality and working skills of the population, increased institutional capacity of public institutes and strengthened the public service capacities dramatically.

IFI Assistance Experiences

During China's economic development over the past twenty years, IFI loans had provided Chinese government the capitals they needed to a certain degree. More importantly, together with the capital and projects, IFIs brought to China new system arrangement, innovation in development viewpoint, knowledge and technologies, as well as management experience. All these knowledge and experience had very important demonstration effects and guiding effects.

The success of development strategy is the greatest success. As the largest developing country in the world, although in absolute number the amount of loans that China received from IFIs is tremendous, the per capita assistance loan received is very small and only accounts for a very small percentage in the total domestic investment. One of the important experiences in China's success is that both the IFIs and China developed feasible development strategies to address development challenges that China faced during different stages in development. Projects are selected under the guidance of the development strategy. In turn, the development assistance strategies are achieved through the successful implementation of projects. Through the spread and dissemination of successful experience, IFIs had played a role of propeller in China's transition from a pro-growth development to a new development viewpoint of putting people first.

Strengthen the combination between loan projects and assistance strategy of IFIs and the multiple development targets of the Chinese government. The assistance projects need to match with the China's development objectives. From China's experience it can be found that the reform and restructuring policies and external assistance are complementary to each other, which will effectively increase the externalities of the development assistance. A typical case would be the introduction of tolling system to the highway projects.

As a recipient, China has been on the driver's seat and designed all the assistance activities to serve its own needs. To get IFI loan is not an objective but a way to achieve development. The objective of Chinese government is not to acquire more capital but to benefit people and economic development of the country through the implementation of the projects. As a recipient, the Chinese government should be the driver and all the activities should serve its own needs. China should adopt an active learning attitude towards IFI development research and policy recommendations and should not follow blindly. We should study carefully as opposed to copy indiscriminately, absorb and experiment with more innovations and play a leading role in project design and execution. In the end, to make the loan projects serve the development strategy of the Chinese government. This is a consumer demand-lead strategy and a development-lead strategy. Drawing on both the international and China's experience, all the international development assistance or projects must fit the local situation, and need to be designed by the recipient country based on actual situation. In the meantime, all the stakeholders, especially the poor should be encouraged to participate in and support the projects. The project regions and targeted groups should really benefit from the projects.

Focus on the system construction and system innovation. IFIs attached great importance to the cross-sector capacity construction using projects, especially strengthened the comprehensive capacity that would improve human resources development and sustainable development. IFIs have always emphasized on establishing effective project financial management system to assist the effective operation of the projects, establishing a set of performance indicators to enhance project monitoring and supervision, evaluating the project performance and establishing project database to lay foundation for project knowledge dissemination. The projects are designed to achieve development, implement a strategy and policies rather than just to build a physical project. Experience shows that IFIs assisted recipient country effectively in making use of global knowledge resources and improving externalities of the project.

Issues and Policy Recommendations

Based on the investigation of the IFI loan projects, we found the following issues in the process of project preparation, construction and management: (1) insufficient understanding of some regions and departments over projects costs and benefits, as well as the risks associated with loan projects; (2) insufficient analysis during project preparation and design. The over-estimated return and extreme long-project construction cycle exposed the projects to policy and exchange risks; (3) lack of management coordination among responsible agencies; (4) in some project entities, the financial system is not well established, and there are cases of violating financial management disciplines and loan agreements; (5) post project work is not enough, such as post-evaluation; (6) sustainability of the projects need to be strengthened.

In regard to the present situation and issues in relation to IFI loan projects, the following policy recommendations were made:

Continue making efficient use of IFI loans. There are great disparities among regions in China, over 2/3 of the regions still need large amount of development assistance. In this process, the transfer payment from central government to local governments needs to be tied with IFI loans to effectively improve the efficiency of capital. In the meantime, to continue to use assistance in developed regions will help China make effective use of global resources.

Actively explore new ways for international cooperation and share China's development achievements with the rest of the world. China needs to coordinate the activities of IFIs and encourage more effective and creative financing models. The government should actively support the international cooperation among IFIs, Chinese NGOs and civil societies, and work with IFIs to assist China to meet the commitments of WTO and complete the accession process successfully.

Promote the change from assistance-lead development to market-based development. Chinese government should make use of the IFI resources, provide services for private enterprises in making use of IFI capital and knowledge and help Chinese enterprises "go out of the country".

The allocation of loans should fit with public investment structure of different regions and favor western and central regions. The public investment requirements of the government should be different in regard to different sectors and regions. Since the western and central regions do not get sufficient funding from government, IFI loans should be mainly used in central and western regions.

To promote the investment system reform in China through IFI loans. To strengthen project execution management and implement investment system of "investor responsibility", namely whoever makes the investment, who will prepare the project, make decision, repay the loan and be responsible. Thus to avoid a phenomenon of "investor missing", that is, one institution is responsible for debt repayment, while the other institution is making the investment decisions.

To further improve the IFI loan projects system construction. Various project preparation systems, management mechanism, supervision and demonstration systems need to be established strictly. These systems cover a series of activities including project feasibility study, organizational and institutional establishment, distribution of responsibilities, matching incentive system, coordination between plan and risks and getting coordinative management of various levels of entities and government ministries. A third-party supervision system needs to be improved at different levels and in different project execution phases.

Actively explore new ways of international cooperation with IFIs in the new era. China should introduce and disseminate China's experience, especially in technology progress, policy options, human resources development, system construction and innovation to other developing countries to make knowledge contribution to the economic growth, structural transition, social development and sustainable development of developing countries.

References

[1] Li Lanqing. Interview with Li Lanqing on Education. Beijing: People's Education Press, 2003. p.19

[2] Asian Development Bank. China Country Strategy and Program (2004 – 2006). November 2003

[3] Liu Qianglun, Wang Taili. Deng Xiaoping's Outstanding Wisdom. Beijing: Contemporary China Press, 2001. pp.56 – 57

Contents

1 Background and Summary

1.1 China Development Context

Since the reform and opening to the outside world in 1978, China has made great achievements in social and economic development and maintained a high growth rate. Gross domestic product (GDP) grew by 9.3% per annum from 1978 to 2003. In the meantime, Chinese economy sustained macro-economic stability, the economic fluctuation coefficient maintained at 33% during 1978 – 2003, while such coefficient was as high as 154% during planned economy era before reform (from 1953 to 1978). In the context of globalization and open market, China successfully withstood various external shocks and emerged one of the best performing economies[①][1]. Average per capita income increased dramatically and poverty population was reduced significantly (Table 1.1). China has successfully transformed from a planned economy to a modern market-based economy. The urbanization process accelerated with the urban population increasing from 173 million in 1978 to over 500 million in 2003. With the policy of opening to the outside world and trade liberalization, China increased its participation in the globalization process. Within one generation, as the largest developing country, China has created an economic development miracle. The World Bank praised China as the most successful developing country in the past two decades. Its successful story brings precious lessons and experiences that can be shared with the rest of the developing world[2].

Generally speaking, China has made four major contributions to the global development:

Growth Contribution. China's total economy growth in 2002 was 9.3 times of that in 1978, average annual growth rate was 9.3% which was more than three times of the world average annual growth during the same period of time. The percentage of Chinese GDP in the world total increased dramatically. China made the second largest contribution to the world GDP increment. Based on the data of Angus Maddison (2001) and in 1990 constant dollars and real purchasing power parity (PPP) terms, the calculation shows that in 1978 China's GDP was 4.9% of the world total GDP, and in 1998, was 11.5% of the world total (Fig. 1.1).

---

① According to the World Bank, since 1997, China has managed macroeconomic conditions well. It has relied on stimulatory macroeconomic policies and a stable exchange rate to sustain domestic demand and activity and support structure reform. Economic performance during 1997 – 2001 was among the best in the world. January 2003, World Bank, China Country Assistance Strategy (2003 – 2005).

During 1980 – 1998, the contribution rate of China's GDP increment to the world GDP increment was 20.6%, while the contribution rate of USA was 23.1% and 7.1% for India[1][3].

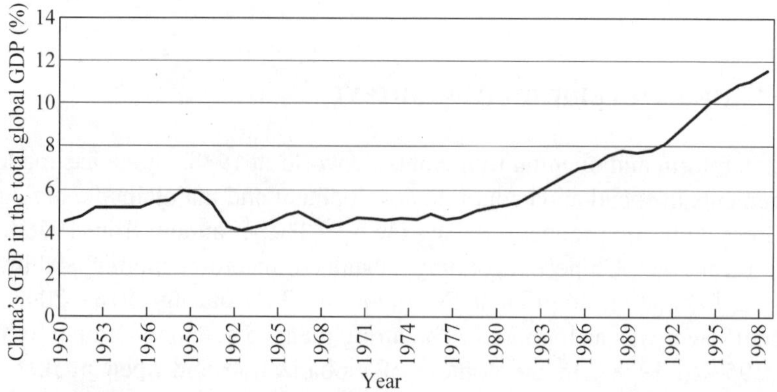

Figure 1.1 Percentage of China's GDP in the total global GDP

Trade Contribution. In 2003, Chinese international trade totaled to US$850 billion, which was 43 times of that in 1978. With an average annual increase rate of 16%, China became the fourth largest trading nation. The ratio of export in GDP as well as the ratio of product export in total export kept rising (Table 1.1). In the meantime, China was the largest recipient of FDI. According to current dollar, from 1978 to 2000, the contribution rate of China to the world new export increment was 4.5% and the contribution rate was 6.5% from 1990 to 2000. The total export of China in the total world export increased from 0.97% in 1978 to 3.96% in 2000, which is estimated to increase to 5% in 2003. While US during 1870 – 1913 and Japan during 1952 – 1995, emerged as big export countries, the share of China's export in the world total export will continue to increase. According to the World Bank, China is one of the most successful globalizers[2][4] by the World Bank[5].

Poverty Reduction Contributions. Poverty population in China has been reduced dramatically from 490 million in 1980 to 200 million in 2000 and poverty incidence rate was reduced from 51% to 16% (Table 1.1). China has achieved many targets set in the Millennium Development Goals of the United Nations ahead of schedule. Among them, the PRC has successfully achieved the key target of halving poverty from the level of 1990. The proportion of the rural population with an income below $1 per day was 31.3% in 1990 and declined to

① Calculation based on the data by Angus Maddison, The World Economy: A Millennium Perspective, OECD, 2001.

② "Globalizers" referred to developing countries that benefited substantially from increasing international trade and foreign direct investment since 1980.

11.5% in 2000. Other Millennium Development Goals, like increasing elementary and junior high school education enrollment rate and reducing maternity and infant morality rate were achieved or largely achieved by 2002 (Table 1.1). In the past two decades, the poverty population reduced in China accounted for 75% of the world total poverty population reduction.

Table 1.1 China major development indicators (1980 – 2002)

	1980	1990	1995	2000	2001	2002
Total population (million)	981	1135	1205	1262	1272	1281
Per capita GDP (in 1995 US$)	167	350	581	825	878	940
Per capita GNI (PPP, current US$)	430	1300	2460	3690	3950	4390
Commodities and service exports (US$ billion)	14	62	168	280	299	386
Export (% of GDP)	8	18	24	26	26	30
Product export (% of total export)	50	74	86	90	90	
Domestic saving (%)	35	38	43	39	40	40
Total capital formulation (%)	35	35	41	36	38	39
Fiscal budget balance (% of GDP)		– 1.9	– 1.7	– 3.6	– 3.3	– 3
Fiscal revenue (% of GDP)	26	20	11	15	17	18.5
External debt (US$ billion)		55	118	146	170	169
Foreign reserve (US$ billion)	2	29	105	166	212	283
Poverty population (million)	490	375	212	204		
Poverty incidence rate (%)	51	33	17	16		

Source: World Bank, World Development Indicators; State Statistics Bureau: *China Statistics Yearbook* (multi years).

Development Experience Contribution. Two decades ago, China was still a low income developing country. At that time, China's per capita GDP was only half of the average level of the low income countries. Most seriously, the development level of agriculture, energy and transportation sectors was very low, the technologies, management and operation of the enterprises were out of date, enterprises are short of skilled workers and technical personnel, illiterate and half illiterate population accounted for one-third of total population and there were hundreds of millions of people living in poverty. Without basic development and transition experience to draw upon, China had to adopt a step-by-step reform strategy of one learns as one goes. After two decades' reform, China emerged from a low income developing country into a lower-medium income country. China had provided other developing countries and transition economies with extensive experiences in poverty reduction, economic growth and social development (Box 1.1).

Box 1.1 A World Bank summary of China's reform and development experience

The success of China's reform provides valuable experiences for other developing countries that are attempting to reform and participate in the globalization process.

Build on existing institutions. The Chinese experience shows that an adaptive process of transition and proceeding step by step, can retain the social and organizational capital developed in previous stages of development and transform it in a way that enhance efficiency and productivity.

Adopt a learning model. Reform is a process of constant learning and adaptation. One learns as one goes. China has successfully allowed regions to experiment and then has scaled up the most successful experiments to the national level.

Recognize the nonlinearity and complexity of reform and change. The reform path may be more zigzag than linear, and China has shown the recognition that changing circumstances requires shifts in approach. Effective systems during certain period of time may not be suitable during other period of time thus require changes accordingly.

Maintain social cohesion. Change can impose strains on a society and it is important to maintain a level of social cohesion that allows people to continue to act together. The Chinese leaders have noticed the balance among reform, development and stabilization.

Source: 2002, Jin Liqun, Nicholas Stern, China Reform Agenda, An Understanding of the World Bank, Economic Development: *Theories and Practises*, Economic Science Publication, 247 – 249.

1.2 Background Review of China Using IFI Loans

In 1978, China was a closed self-sufficient and self-reliance less developed economy with limited economic activities with the rest of the world. The share of total Chinese export in the world total export plumped to less than 1%, which was the lowest in history, even lower than 2.5% in 1870[6]. China was one of the few economies that had neither domestic nor external debt[7]. In 1978, at the third session of the Eleventh National Congress of the Communist Party of China, it was pointed out clearly for the first time to "actively promote equal and mutually beneficial economic cooperation with other countries based on the principle of self-reliance and try to adopt advanced technology and equipments". Deng Xiaoping, with great vision, made a very important decision to actively utilize foreign capital. In October 1978, Deng Xiaoping visited Japan, and the same November visited Thailand, Malaysia and Singapore during which he showed great interest in learning experiences on attracting foreign investment and introducing advanced technologies. Later, in January 1979, Deng Xiaoping visited Huston and Seattle during his official visit to the United States and learned the economic development, science and technology, culture and education in the United States and made up his mind to take "opening to the outside world" as our basic policy. At the end of 1979, strongly promoted by Deng Xiaoping, the National Committee of Foreign Investment Management was established. Gu Mu, Vice Prime Minister, was the Director General of the Committee and Jiang Zemin as Secretary. Li Lanqing was put in charge of the World Bank and other foreign loans. Before our reform and opening to the outside world, many developing countries including India and Pakistan have received substantial amount of soft loans (zero-interest loans) from IFIs, such as the World Bank. These loans had played significant roles in the economic development of these countries. After careful research and study, the National Committee of Foreign Investment Management reported the findings to the Central Government. The Central Government decided that China would join the World Bank and establish formal financial cooperation relationships with related countries[8]. At that time, the guiding idea of utilizing foreign capital is to use foreign loans rather than foreign direct investment. The foreign loans are mainly inter-government loans and medium and long-term loans from IFIs.

In May 1980, World Bank resumed China's member status and right as loan recipient. This is a very important start for China to get rid of the long-standing isolationism and open to the outside world. Just as Deng Xiaoping pointed out that "without the assistance from the World Bank we can do, but with your help, we can develop a bit faster". And as mentioned by Mr. McNamara, the President of the World Bank at the time, that one of the achievements that he was proud of the most during his office was to take China back as a member when China just began its reform and opening to the outside world at early 1980s.

1.3 An Overview and General Evaluation of China Attracting IFI Loans

From 1981 to 2002, China has received US$62 billion loans from IFIs in total accumulation, among which the total World Bank loan is US$36.6 billion, the total ADB loan is US$12.16 billion, International Financial Corporation (IFC) loan is US$1.27 billion and total International Fund for Agriculture Development (IFAD) is US$430 million. By 2002, China has become one of the major borrowers of the World Bank. The total borrowing from the World Bank accounted over half of the total loans of IFIs to China. From the establishment of the World Bank till June of 2001, the World Bank had provided a total loan of US$487 billion for developing countries. China's borrowing accounted for 7.5% of the total lending of the World Bank. Refer to Table 1.2 for detailed information regarding total accumulated IFI loan and number of projects. Most of the loans were used in strategic sectors and areas that require longer term of investment cycle and had greater social benefits and profound influence on development, such as agriculture and rural development, infrastructure, education, health, environment protection and poverty reduction. These sectors are public investment sectors that foreign private investors are unlikely to participate.

Table 1.2 Overview of IFI capital and project

Institution	Time period	Accumulated capital (100 million US$)	No. of projects	Projects in construction	Key assistance sectors
World Bank	1981 – 2002	366.0	245	90	Transportation (29%) Agriculture, forestry (23%) Energy (18%)
ADB	1986 – 2002	122.0	91		Transportation (49.3%) Energy (17.3%) Social infrastructure (7.9)
IFC		12.7			
IFAD		4.3			
IFI	1981 – 2000	620.0			

Note: the number in the parentheses is the percentage of loans of this sector in the total loans.

IFI assistance loans to China has the following characteristics: (1) the total loan to China is the largest[①][9], while the per capita loan is pretty small[②]; (2) the percentages of loan in total domestic investment and GDP are pretty low despite the large size of the total loans[③][10] (Table 1.3); (3) the trend of IFI loans in total foreign trade followed a pattern of increase followed by decrease, while foreign direct investment kept increasing and became major source for foreign capital (Table 1.3) and (4) assistance is not only limited to investment, but also includes technical assistance, policy advisory, project consultancy, human resources training, international experience and knowledge learning, etc. Although IFIs only provided assistance for China for 22 years, their operations are very successful. China's reform and opening to the outside world had improved domestic environment

① China is No. 1 borrower in the World Bank in terms of loan amount; China portfolio is one of ADB's largest and best performing portfolios, China portfolio accounted 12% of ADB total portfolio.

② China's total amount of official development assistance is large, but the per capita assistance amount and the weight to GDP are not high. Regarding the per capita assistance amount, China was US$2, while Pakistan was US$5, Uzbekistan was US$6, Viet Nam was US$13, Cambodia was US$36, Mongolia was US$99; The weight of assistance to GDP: China was 0.2%, other countries ranged from 4.1% to 26.7%. China is the lowest per capita assistance recipient country among the 7 countries who received regional technical assistance.

③ The ratio of official development assistance funds to government spending was less than 1.5%, to total fixed assets investment was less than 0.7%.

Table 1.3 International assistance loans and FDI during different time periods

Item	Sixth five-year plan 1981 – 1985	Seventh five-year plan 1986 – 1990	Eighth five-year plan 1991 – 1995	Ninth five-year plan 1996 – 2000
Assistance loan (US$100 million)	39.60	128.20	217.03	235.23
Assistant loan over total foreign capital (%)	26.21	27.70	13.47	8.12
Assistance loan over GDP (%)	0.08	0.30	0.33	0.22
FDI (US$100 million)	45.63	142.62	1141.80	2134.80
FDI over total foreign capital (%)	30.20	30.81	7.89	73.67
FDI over GDP (%)	0.30	0.77	3.92	4.53

Source: Ministry of Foreign Trade and Economic Cooperation, *China Yearbook of Foreign Trade and Economic Cooperation* (multi-years), Beijing, Foreign Trade Press.

substantially and capacity in utilizing loans, project implementation and development. The combination of external assistance and internal capital, the inter-support and inter-conformation of external recommendations with internal reform contributed to the successful operation of IFI assistance. According to the statistics of Center for Global Development (2003), in 74 international assistance recipient economies, the average percentage of assistance received is 10.8% of GDP, while the 28 nations whose per capita GNI is between US$1,435 and US$2,975, the percentage of assistance received is 1.4% of GDP① [11]. In comparison, China is a low income country with low percentage of international assistance in total GDP, however, the development performance is one of the best in the world[12] (Table 1.4).

Over the past two decades, China has always been one of the largest recipients of the IFIs. The total project capitals amounted to RMB1,000 billion, among which the World Bank and ADB loans accounted for 40%②, around RMB406 billion. IFIs have provided very effective development assistance in many key sectors in China and played satisfactory roles in promoting and supporting China's reform, opening to the outside world and development.

The overall performance of the assistance projects has been very successful. This study shows, from both macro and micro points of view, that the IFI projects are very successful. Among the total nine sectors reviewed in this study, seven are rated successful which accounted for 78%. The Operations Evaluation Department of the World Bank rated China's operation over the world average level. The evaluation over the projects completed since 1980 proved yet again

① OED of the World Bank thinks the performance of Chinese projects is better than the world average, the satisfactory rates is much higher than the world average. It is further proved by the evaluation to the completed projects after 1980: the unsatisfactory projects in China's portfolio was 9%, the average of the World Bank wide was 31% for the same period.

② Calculated in current exchange rate, data provided by the International Department, Ministry of Finance.

Table 1.4 Comparing development indicators, capital inflow and finance resources (average) among three MCA country groups and China

	Countries that meet IDA requirements and per capita GNI under US$1,435	Countries whose per capita GNI under US$1,435	Countries whose per capita GNI between US$1,435 and US$2,975	China
Development indicators				
Per capita GNI in 2001 ($)	380	460	1965	890
Adult literacy rate in 2000 (%)	36	33	14	16
Life expectancy at birth in 2000 (year)	54	56	70	70
Infant mortality rate (every 1,000 life birth)	75	69	27	32
Capital flow and finance				
Official development assistance 2000 over GNI (%)	10.8	8.5	1.4	0.02
Total private capital inflow over GDP (%)	6.9	8.7	10.3	12.7
Tax income over GDP (%)	11.7	12.6	21.8	6.8
Total domestic saving in 2000 over GDP (%)	7.3	8.4	16.2	39.9
Number of countries	74	87	28	

Source: Steven Radelet, 2003, Challenging Foreign Aid, Center for Global Development, Washington, DC, Table 2.1.

that the rating of many projects are way above world average level: the percentage of projects rated unsatisfactory in China was 9% while the bank-wide average level during the same period was 31%[13]. The Evaluation Report of the ADB concluded that the PRC portfolio is one of ADB's largest and best performing portfolios. The project implementation in China is consistently better than the overall level of the ADB projects. As a loan recipient, China enjoys a good reputation of maintaining high project quality and debt repayment in the world. This proves that Chinese government has very strong project management capability and pretty good internal control system[14].

The role of the World Bank, ADB and other IFIs are no longer limited to lending agencies, and they have become development assistance agencies in a broader sense that promotes the achievement of global Millennium Goals through providing a series of assistances including making investment, supporting system construction, enhancing management capacity, providing policy advisory, global knowledge network and human resources network. Mr Li Lanqing, former Deputy Prime Minister spoke highly of the IFIs and their assistance: "the World Bank and other foreign governments' favorable loans have played very positive roles in our education, personnel training, basic infrastructure construction and enterprise technology renovation[15]." One of the most important significances of receiving loan assistance from IFIs for China is that it helped China smoothly transform from a closed economy and open to the outside world, end China's long-standing isolationism and integrate China with the rest of the world. Mr. Deng Xiaoping had repeatedly emphasized that "opening to the outside world has profound significance. Any nation that wants to develop will not achieve its goal if it isolates itself from the rest of the world. It is impossible for a country to develop without increasing international exchange, learning from advanced experiences and technology and utilizing capital from developed countries[16]." International assistance loans make Deng Xiaoping's idea conceivable.

1.4 Project Background and Methodology

This project is sponsored by International Department, Ministry of Finance. The purpose of this study is for the first time to review and evaluate the 22 years' operation of IFI assistances comprehensively against the general background of Chinese economic development, transition and integration. On the one hand, the study will analyze various benefits of IFIs and their contribution to development; on the other hand, investigate the actual effects and efficacy of individual projects from a micro point of view. The study will draw successful experiences from the cooperation between Chinese government and IFIs, as well as identify and analyze issues and lessons in project management to make guidance and policy recommendations on improving further cooperation and achieving mutual benefits.

It took the Center for China Study one year to conduct theoretical research, investigation and information collection. Over sixty individuals participated in the project during different stages. The center working with the International Department completed a survey in 31 provinces and collected data. We also conducted a core study in 13 provinces involving 53 key projects of nine sectors and submitted related research reports. Project results also include: survey data collection software, IFIs operation evaluation sub-reports (macro and micro), and post-evaluation report.

This study adopted a combined macro and micro analysis methodology on the basis of the theory and actual investigation. Macro analysis adopted a variety of research methodologies related to economics, calculated the (medium and short term) impact and accumulated contribution of IFI loans on growth, private investment increase and FDI increase. In micro analysis, based on investigation and information collected and combined with China's situation, we developed indicator system to make sector evaluation. We also evaluated targets, process (management system, IFI performance, and borrower performance), results and impacts (economic, environmental, social and sustainability) and made relevant policy recommendations.

The World Bank and ADB have provided tremendous help for this project. The final summary report is based on extensive references to their research papers including conclusions and research methodologies, comments and suggestions made by experts①, as well as empirical studies of the domestic and international experts②.

However, owing to the fact that this project involved many complex sectors, and had no previous examples to learn from, the research methods adopted are difficult to identify, the data is insufficient and a large number of it can not be used. There are ample rooms for improvement in our research and report, and we hope that we have laid a foundation for such research in the future.

References

[1] World Bank. China country assistance strategy (2003 – 2005). January 2003

[2] Nicholas Stern, Jin Liqun. Preface, Economic Development: Theory and Practice. Beijing: Economic Science Press, 2002. p.1

[3] Angus Maddison. The world economy: A millennium perspective. OECD, 2001

[4] David Dollar. Globalization, growth and poverty. 2002

[5] Nicholas Stern. Preface, Economic Development: Theory and Practice. Beijing: Economic Science Press, 2002. p.2

[6] Angus Maddison. Chinese economic performance in the long run, OECD, 1996

[7] Li Lanqing. Interview with Li Lanqing on Education. Beijing: People's Education Press, 2003. p.18

[8] Li Lanqing. Interview with Li Lanqing on Education. Beijing: People's Education Press, 2003. pp.18 – 19

[9] ADB: Country strategy and program (2004 – 2006), November 2003

[10] ADB: Country strategy and program (2004 – 2006), November 2003

[11] Steven Radelet. Challenging foreign aid, center for global development, Washington, DC, 2003, Table 2.1

[12] The World Bank Group. China country assistance strategy (2003 – 2005). January 2003; World Bank. China: Country assistance evaluation. Operation evaluation department, December 29, R2003 – 0225, 2003; ADB China country strategy and program (2004 – 2006), November 2003

① The International Department of MOF invited Mr. Wu Ning, Zhang Sanli and Zhang Kaiping to provide comments and recommendations to the study.

② Special thanks to Professor Lu Xiaobo, Columbia University, Dr Zheng Haijing, Goltberg University of Sweden, Professor Wang Shaoguang, Hong Kong University, Dr Chen Xinhua, International Energy Agency, Researcher Lu Zhongyuan, Development Research Center of State Council.

[13] World Bank. China country assistance strategy (2003 – 2005), January 2003; World Bank. China: Country Assistance Evaluation, Operation Evaluation Department, December 29, R2003 – 0225, 2003

[14] ADB. China country strategy and program (2004 – 2006), Novermber 2003

[15] Li Lanqing. Interview with Li Lanqing on Education. Beijing: People's Education Press, 2003. p.19

[16] Liu Qianglun, Wang Taili. Deng Xiaoping's Outstanding Wisdom. Beijing: Contemporary China Press, 2001. pp.56 – 57

2 Objective Evaluation

The post-project evaluation indicator system we use is developed by the Logical Framework Analysis Method (LFA). It unfolds into project objective supposition, process of execution and impact of projects after completion. As the importance of all indicators is different to project execution results, so we have given them different degrees of impact (weighted) in our comprehensive evaluation. Appendix 1 is a detailed introduction of the evaluation framework.

Below, we shall use the above framework to evaluate and analyze the World Bank and Asian Development Bank projects in China from three different logical levels.

2.1 Evaluation Indicator System

Objective evaluation is the evaluation of the objectives established at the time of project proposal stage and the degree of realization. Objectives here refer to the strategic objectives of projects. The objective evaluation is divided into two levels: the first level involves the correctness, rationale and operability of setting of the objectives at the time of project proposal. For some projects, the objectives set are not definite or fail to accord with realities or are too optimistic or too pessimistic about development prospects or encounter major changes in the policy and market environment and require re-evaluation of the objectives set at the time of project proposal in the post-project evaluation. This step is useful in drawing experiences and lessons for future projects. The second level involves the evaluation of the degree of realization of the objectives at the time of or for a period of time after completion. The indicators for judging the degree of realization of the objectives are mainly divided into macro indicators and direct purpose of projects. The macroscopic indicators weigh the general effect and roles of projects on regions, industries and national economic and social development; direct purposes are likely to be products and services provided or the easing of supply and demand conflicts (see Table 2.1).

As the purpose of IFI assistance loans is to help recipient countries develop, the objectives of specific projects are subordinated to the strategic framework of IFIs, especially the World Bank and the Asian Development Bank.

Table 2.1 Objective evaluation indicators and grading

	HS	S	U
Degree of realization of strategic objectives	Full realization of strategic objectives set are completed after completion of projects	The set strategic objectives are basically completed after completion	The set strategic objectives are not realized basically or what has been achieved has serious deviated from the set strategic objectives after completion
Degree of realization of direct purposes	The set direct objecttives are fully realized after completion	Direct objectives set are basically realized after completion	Direct objectives set are basically not realized or what has been achieved has serious deviated from the set objectives after completion
Rationale of direct purposes of projects	Objectives designed in the project feasibility studies totally tally with the development demand of the project area or totally tally with the requirements of the industry of the project	Objectives designed in the project feasibility studies basically tally with the development demand of the project area or basically tally with the requirements of the industry of the project	Objectives designed in the project feasibility studies do not tally with the development demand of the project area or not tally with the requirements of the industry of the project

2.2 Evaluation Results

Of the 47 sample projects, 17 are rated as "highly successful" (HS), accounting for 36%; 24 are rated as "successful"(S), accounting for 51% and six are rated as "unsuccessful" (U), accounting for 13% (see Fig. 2.1). The number of projects successful in general makes up over 85%. This shows that all the sample IFI loan projects have basically realized the set strategic objectives and immediate objectives and the set objectives of most projects are rational.

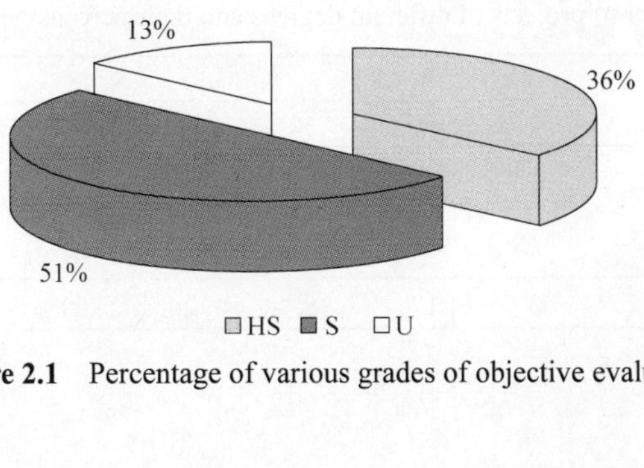

Figure 2.1 Percentage of various grades of objective evaluation

Table 2.2 shows that the objectives of the projects in industry, communications, health, urban construction and environmental protection have been realized satisfactorily without any unsuccessful sample projects. The degree of realization and rationality is the highest with the projects in communications, health and environmental protection, accounting for more than 50% (including 50%) of the sample projects. Projects in energy, education, water supply and environmental health are poor, with unsuccessful projects making up over 25% (including 25%) of the sample projects. Objectives evaluation in different regions shows that the percentage of sample projects that are successful and highly successful in the eastern part is higher than that in the middle and western parts, reaching 92.7%. The percentage of unacceptable projects in the middle part is lower than that in the western part. But in terms of the percentage of the highest degree of objective realization, it is much higher in the western part than in the middle part and even than in the eastern part. Most of the projects in the middle and eastern parts are of medium success (general success level), basically normal. The successful projects in the western part are concentrated in the highest grades (see Table 2.3).

Table 2.2 Number of industry-specific projects of all grades and % in total

	HS		S		U	
	Number	%	Number	%	Number	%
Agriculture	3	18.75	11	68.75	2	12.5
Industry	1	50.00	1	50.00	0	0.0
Energy	1	25.00	2	50.00	1	25.0
Communications	4	66.67	2	33.33	0	0.0
Education	2	33.33	2	33.33	2	33.3
Health	3	50.00	3	50.00	0	0.0
Water supply and environmental health	2	50.00	1	25.00	1	25.0
Urban construction	0	0.00	1	100.00	0	0.0
Environmental protection	1	50.00	1	50.00	0	0.0
Total	17	36	24	51	6	13

Table 2.3 Number of projects of different degrees and their percentage in different regions

	HS		S		U	
	Number	%	Number	%	Number	%
Eastern part	9	37.50	13	54.17	2	8.33
Middle part	1	8.33	9	75.00	2	16.67
Western part	7	60.00	2	20.00	2	20.00
Total	17	36	24	51	6	13

3 Process Evaluation

3.1 Evaluation of Management System

3.1.1 Evaluation Indicators Set

IFIs usually introduce new project management mechanism in most of China loan projects, including project financial management mechanism, project process oversight system, project organizational setup and project evaluation models. The practice of the past nearly 20 years shows that the project management system is closely related with project success. The management system and model have gradually been integrated with the realities in China through the 20 years practice and helped improve the China project management. They have also had a far-reaching significance in all aspects of China including institutional development and organizational reforms. That is why many project proposal reports include institutional innovation and performances as fairly important objectives of projects.

First of all, institutional development impact is to study the impact and degree of promotion of a project on human, capital and natural resources of a country or a region. The institutional development impact of a project is realized mainly by strengthening the implications of new institutional arrangements, contents, stability, transparency, coerciveness and predictability or through enhancing the understanding of the public of organizational or institutional tasks and capabilities. In the process of the operation of projects, institutional development impact may have specific results and additional results. The former is the objective for defining institutional construction and overflow of projects themselves, such as some technical assistance projects, which have an independent part on institutional construction. The latter refers to social demonstrative efficiency and leading efficiency resulting from the remarkable institutional construction in the process of project implementation.

Institutional development exerts its influence by changing the management system and the macro system. This can be divided into the following three indicators:

Whether or not there are new institutional arrangements in the process of the operation of the projects, such as introduction of new laws and regulations, incentive mechanisms and competitive rules or new establishments or dismissals or reform or improvements, introduction of information system and improvement in policy analysis.

Whether or not the new institutional arrangements have demonstrative effect, such as duplicability or applicability in the management and operation of other projects.

Whether or not the implementation of projects has uniformity, for instance whether or not project implementing units have changed in the process of operation or whether or not the project units have changed.

Our investigations are centered on the above three indicators. In the process of evaluation, we rate each indicator as highly successful (HS), successful (S) and unsuccessful (U). The specifics are shown in the following Table 3.1.

Table 3.1 Evaluation indicators and grades of management system

	HS	S	U
Institutional arrangements	New institutional arrangements introduced and they play an important role in project operation	New institutional arrangements introduced and they play a certain role in project operation	No new institutional arrangements introduced or institutional arrangements introduced fail to play any roles in project operation
Demonstrative effect	Institutional arrangements introduced play a demonstrative role for similar projects and feature duplicability, and applicability in other projects	Institutional arrangements introduced have certain degree of duplicability and reference value and may serve as a reference for similar projects	Institutional arrangements introduced has sole applicability and cannot serve as reference for similar projects
Uniformity of operation	Project implementation units and project management units have kept pace from the very beginning	Project implementing units are consistent, but project management units altered or changes have taken place with project implementing units but project management units are consistent	Changes have taken place in both project implementation and management units

3.1.2 Evaluation Results

(1) In general the institutional performance is satisfactory. Twelve projects are rated as highly successful, accounting for 53% and projects above the successful grading make up 88%. The specific distribution is shown in Fig. 3.1. This shows that we have introduced a lot of new institutional arrangements favorable for the operation of projects in utilizing IFI loans. At the same time, these institutional

arrangements have strong demonstrative effect and provided valuable experience for the operation of similar projects, including institutional arrangements and management supervision, thus playing an important role in the smooth implementation of projects. We may also discover that the main factor leading to unsuccessful projects is the inconsistency of project management units and project implementation units.

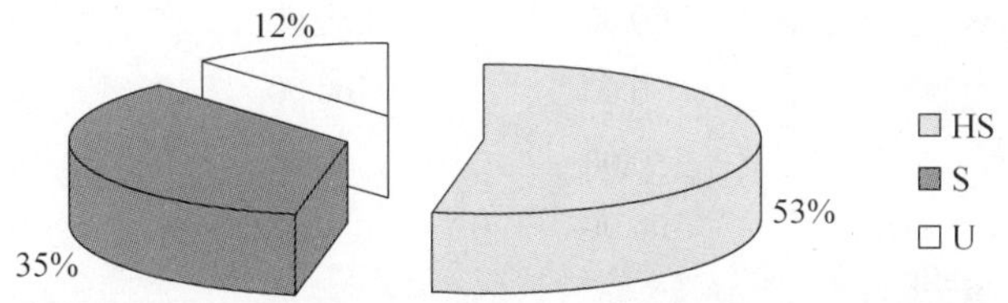

Figure 3.1 Proportion of all grades in performance evaluation

(2) The number of highly successful projects in all regions is identical, basically staying at about 50%, as shown in Fig. 3.2, with that in the western part being the highest and that of in the middle part poorer than in the eastern and western part. Most of the projects with poor performances are concentrated in the middle part, accounting for about 40% of the total projects.

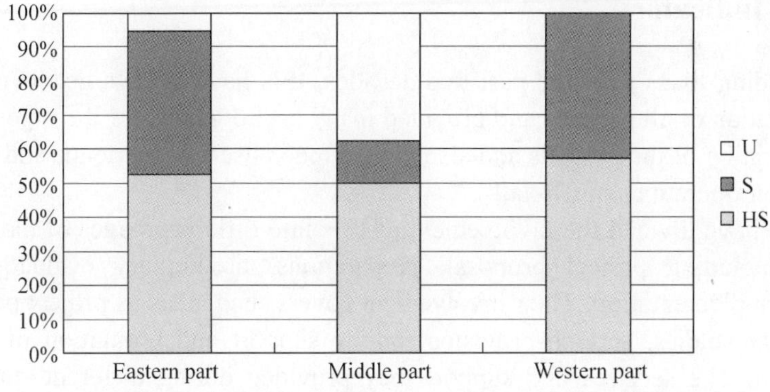

Figure 3.2 Regional comparison in project performances

(3) In terms of industry, projects in agriculture, water supply, health and urban health and other public utility industries are highly successful. Of the 15 agricultural projects surveyed, 10 are highly successful, which constitute two-thirds of the total agricultural projects. The projects in these industries have benefited from the introduction of institutional innovation while the performances of projects in energy, communications and education are ordinary, as shown in Table 3.2.

Table 3.2 Comparison of sample project industries

	HS		S		U		Total
	Number	%	Number	%	Number	%	Number
Agriculture	10	66.67	4	26.67	1	6.67	15
Industry	1	50.00	1	50.00	0	0.00	2
Energy	1	25.00	2	50.00	1	25.00	4
Communications	0	0.00	1	50.00	1	50.00	2
Education	0	0.00	2	100.00	0	0.00	2
Health	2	50.00	2	50.00	0	0.00	4
Water supply and environmental health	2	100.00	0	0.00	0	0.00	2
Urban construction	1	100.00	0	0.00	0	0.00	1
Environmental protection	1	50.00	0	0.00	1	50.00	2

3.2 Evaluation of IFI Performance

3.2.1 Indicators

In providing loans over the past two decades, IFIs have always got involved in the operation of all projects and provided many useful guides for the organization and operation of the projects and also gained much useful experience and lessons from their operations in China.

We have divided the involvement of IFIs into different stages of the project cycle, including project proposal, preparations, preliminary evaluation and project implementation. Their involvement covers such areas as project proposal, feasibility studies, service provision, policy support and regulation of project operation. The services and support they provided during different stages are different.

In the project proposal and preparation stage, their support and services include advancing their requirements, strategic objectives, project objectives and project operational methods, helping project implementation units set up corresponding systems and rules and providing them with experience of related projects for reference.

In the project implementation stage, IFIs mainly provide services for the implementation of projects and carry out supervision and evaluation of projects during operation and adjustment of project indicators, including the improvement of systems and rules, financial affairs supervision and technical assistance.

In general, IFIs played an active part in the implementation of all loan projects by way of setting up special archives for projects and taking charge of expert group and many other ways including carrying out investigations and study, training, process evaluation, supervision and financial affairs control. Most project implementation units deem the active participation of IFIs essential for the smooth-going of the projects and they have learned a lot of management methods and experience from international experts during the operation of the projects. We have studied, through investigations and interviews, their involvement in the process of project proposal, mid-term adjustment, technical assistance and process control and grade them in HS, S and U. The specifics are shown in Table 3.3.

Table 3.3 Grading indicators and evaluation grades of the performance of international financial institutions

	HS	S	U
Involvement in project proposal	Involvement of lenders in project proposal advancement, feasibility studies and preliminary evaluation	No involvement of lenders in project proposal advancement, but involvement in feasibility studies and preliminary evaluation after projects are approved	No involvement in project proposal advancement, feasibility studies and preliminary evaluation or the involvement in these process fail to play a guiding role
Mid-term adjustment	In the process of project operation, lenders directed project implementation units to make effective mid-term adjustment, thus reducing losses of efficiency	In the process of project operation, lenders directed project implementation units to make timely mid-term adjustment and the adjustment failed to achieve better results	In the process of project operation, lenders fail to make effective mid-term adjustment timely according to the operation of projects
Technical assistance and process control	In the process of project operation, lenders sent experts to provide guidance for project management and technical progress and carried out effective control of the operations	In the process of project operation, lenders sent experts to provide guidance for project management and technical progress, although the guidance played little role in it	In the process of project operation, lenders failed to send experts to provide guidance

3.2.2 Sample Evaluation

(1) In general, the involvement of IFIs is not so satisfactory (Fig. 3.3). The number of highly successful projects accounted for less than 20%. Two-fifth of the projects show that the involvement performance of IFIs is poor. The three major indicators show that IFIs practically did not get involved in writing project proposal reports and feasibility studies. This led to a large scaled mid-term adjustment to respond to market changes and policy impact.

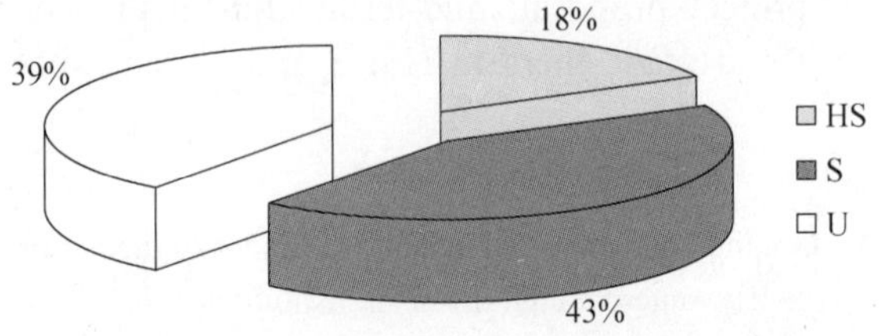

Figure 3.3 Grading of involvement of IFIs

(2) In terms of regions, as shown in Fig. 3.4, involvement of IFIs in the project in the eastern part is high, with the number of projects rated above "successful" reaching 70% in the eastern part and also nearly 60% in the western part. But IFI involvement in project in the middle part is poor, with the degree of less than 50%.

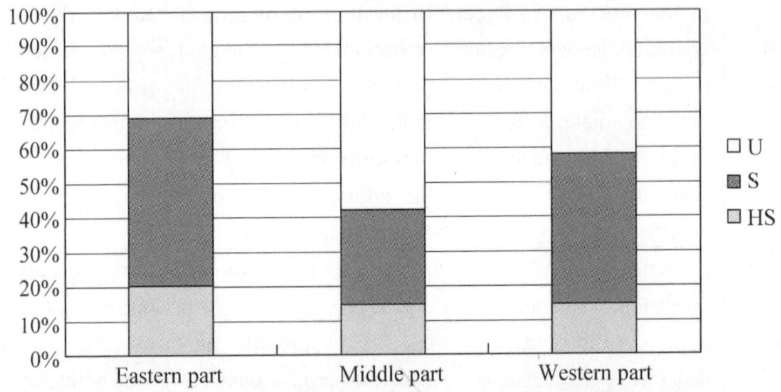

Figure 3.4 Regional comparison of involvement of IFIs

(3) In terms of industrial distribution, IFIs are fairly successful in their involvement in such industries as energy, education and health projects, but poor in industry, communications and urban construction. The main factors accounting for this is lack of project proposal advancement and feasibility studies. As shown in Table 3.4.

Table 3.4 Comparison of sample project sectors

	HS		S		U		Total
	Number	%	Number	%	Number	%	Number
Agriculture	4	28.57	5	35.71	5	35.71	14
Industry	0	0.00	1	50.00	1	50.00	2
Energy	1	25.00	2	50.00	1	25.00	4
Communications	0	0.00	1	50.00	1	50.00	2
Education	1	50.00	1	50.00	0	0.00	2
Health	0	0.00	3	75.00	1	25.00	4
Water supply and environmental health	0	0.00	1	50.00	1	50.00	2
Urban construction	0	0.00	0	0.00	1	100.00	1
Environmental protection	0	0.00	1	50.00	1	50.00	2

3.3 Evaluation of the Performances of Lenders

3.3.1 Evaluation Indicators

Before evaluating the involvement of lenders, we first of all define the scope of lenders. Here lenders are a general term for project implementation units and project management units. IFI project loans are basically governmental loans, with loans borrowed by state finance or provincial level finance with government credit as the gurarantee and then are re-loaned to projects. Therefore during the operation of a project which is implemented by financial departments. In a low level or other government departments in charge of operating such projects and, while national organizations or provincial governments who have obtained the loans. The two are often not identical. But in our evaluation, we treat them differently as the two are different in the impact of the operations of the projects.

Involvement of lenders refers to the involvement in the entire operational cycle of projects, including project design, preparations, quality of implementation and efforts toward the performance of contracts, agreement and sustainability of projects. The tasks of project units are mainly to coordinate steps to ensure smooth-going of projects and coordinate multi-sector cooperation. The tasks of project implementation units are to promote and publicize projects and stimulate the operation of projects, but they are not in the capacity of demanding matching funds to be put in place or paying back the loans. It is a process of cooperation between the two kinds of units. So our evaluation mainly focuses on the amount of matching funds and disbursement, the efforts made by lenders in project promotion and operation and loan repayment mechanism. We also rate them in three grades: HS, S and U. The specifics as shown in the following Table 3.5.

Table 3.5 Evaluation indictors and grades of the performances of lenders

	HS	S	U
Matching funds	Amount of matching funds and proportion have met the requirements of projects and have been put in place timely	Amount of matching funds and proportion have met the requirements of projects but have not been put in place timely	Amount of matching funds and proportion have not met the requirements of projects
Efforts made	Lenders have done a lot of publicity for project promotion and operation, encouraged local people to get involved and provided guidance for project operations by technical extension and training	Lenders have done a lot of publicity for project promotion and operation and carried out activities for providing guidance for project operations	Lenders have not done any publicity for project promotion and operation or have not paid enough attention to the operation of the projects
Loan repayment mechanism	Lenders have done enough publicity of project loan repayment and established an effective loan repayment mechanism	Lenders have established a certain loan repayment mechanism	Lenders have not established any loan repayment mechanism

3.3.2 Result of Evaluation

(1) In general, involvement of lenders is not optimistic. The number of projects with poor lender involvement accounted for 50% and projects with highly successful involvement accounted for only 6% (Fig. 3.5). This shows that there is much to do for project units and project implementation units. Specific indicators

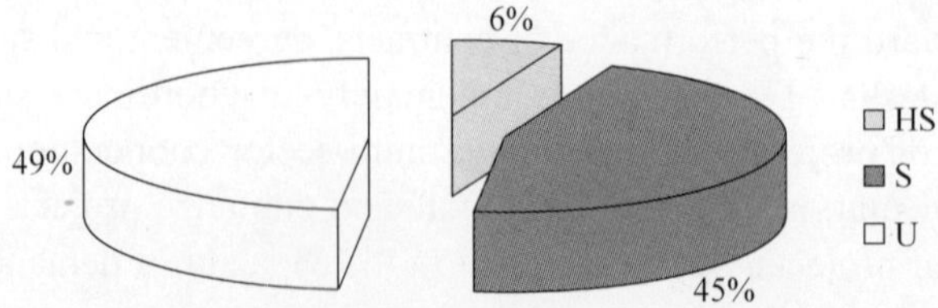

Figure 3.5 Involvement of lenders and their grading

show that a serious problem is that matching funds could not be put in place. In addition, project units and project implementation units have a weak sense of loan repayment, which lead to poor repayment of loans.

(2) In term of regions, the performances of lenders in the middle part are poor, with the unsatisfactory lender involvement reaching more than 70%. The situation is the same in the eastern and western parts, with the unsatisfactory lender involvement reaching 40% (Fig. 3.6).

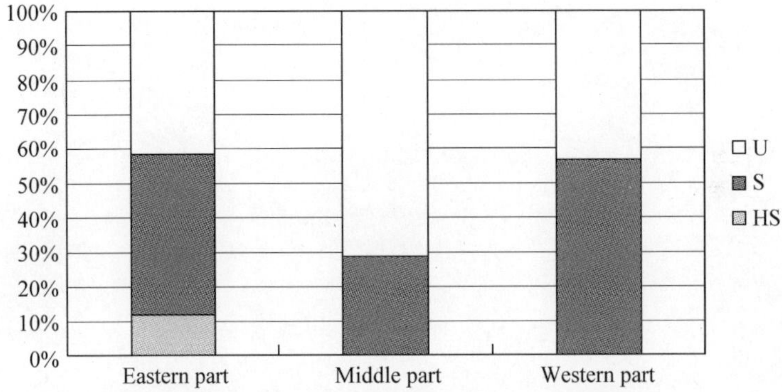

Figure 3.6 Regional comparison of lender involvement

(3) In terms of different sectors, the lender performances in agricultural, water supply and environmental health projects are relatively poor but in communications and education are not bad. The specifics as shown in the following Table 3.6.

Table 3.6 Comparison of sample project sectors

	HS		S		U		Total
	Number	%	Number	%	Number	%	Number
Agriculture	2	14.29	4	28.57	8	57.14	14
Industry	0	0.00	1	50.00	1	50.00	2
Energy	0	0.00	2	66.67	1	33.33	3
Communications	0	0.00	2	100.00	0	0.00	2
Education	0	0.00	2	100.00	0	0.00	2
Health	0	0.00	2	66.50	1	33.50	3
Water supply and environmental health	0	0.00	0	0.00	2	100.00	2
Urban construction	0	0.00	0	0.00	1	100.00	1
Environmental protection	0	0.00	1	50.00	1	50.00	2

The above three factors show that process control is good only in energy and education projects, because project management systems of the two sectors are strict, processes are easy to control and project units and project implementation units are unified. The process control in most other sectors is not so satisfactory, which owing to many factors. The main factor is that the actual person and investor are not unified, the coordinating mechanism is not flexible and effective, and institutional reforms lead to lack of project leader and project implementer.

4 Evaluation of Results and Impact

4.1 Macro Economic Evaluation

Since 1981, funds of US$27.351 billion have flowed into China from international financial institutions (IFIs), accounting for 5.34% of the capital inflow. The World Bank and the Asian Development Bank are the two multilateral development organizations that have provided the most loans to China. But have these loans had any impact on China's economic growth and on absorbing foreign private capital? How should a macro evaluation be made quantitatively? This paper tries to use, for the first time, a macroeconometric model to evaluate the economic impact of the IFI loans by exploiting the latest development of assistance loan theories and the innovation of the quantitative method. Study result shows that the use of IFI loans is the starting point and a very important component part of China's opening to the outside world and has had positive impact on many aspects. It has had a strong inducement effect on China's economic growth, private investment and international direct investment (FDI). The multiplication effect of the loan investment is also significant. In the middle and western parts of the country, IFI loans have directly stimulated economic growth and had a balancing effect on narrowing the gaps between the eastern part of the country and the middle and western parts. In the eastern part, it has directly stimulated private investment and FDI by improving investment environment, thus indirectly stimulating economic growth. It has also played a supporting role in the transition of public investors and government consumption. On the other hand, our study has also shown that there is much room for improvement in the use of IFI loans, especially in the even regional development and in financial system transition.

4.1.1 Background and Method of the Study

More than two decades ago, China was an underdeveloped, self-sufficient country with little contact with other economies in the world. It was among a few countries that had neither domestic nor foreign debts. After the 3rd session of the 11th Party Central Committee in 1978, Deng Xiaoping took the major policy decision of actively utilizing foreign capital, and a foreign investment management committee of China was set up. From then on, the country began to consider using loans from international financial institutions. In 1980, the World

Bank began to restore China's position and rights to loans as a member. Just as Deng Xiaoping said, "We can go with or without you. But with your assistance, we may go faster in development." Since then, China began to open the door. The opening up started with accepting loans and assistance from international financial institutions when China was seriously short of funds for economic development and lack of the conditions to attract FDI. China was in urgent need of building energy and infrastructure projects, developing agriculture and rural economy and reducing the poor population. Although IFI loans took only a small part in GDP and domestic investment, they were timely, just like offering fuel in snowy weather as the Chinese saying goes.

During 1981 – 2000, China accepted US$62 billion of assistance loans from IFIs. The World Bank had provided US$34.2 billion loans by the end of 2002, which were used to support 259 projects, of which 157 have been completed. China has thus become the biggest debtor country of the World Bank, with more than half of the total assistance loans from international financial institutions. The Bank's assistance loans to China made up about 7.5% of the total US$487 billion provided to developing countries since its setup in June 2001. The Asian Development Bank provided China with US$12.2 billion from 1987 to the end of 2000, next only to the World Bank. The money was used to fund 91 projects. The loans provided to China made up 12% of the total loans dispensed by the Asian Development Bank[1].

Table 4.1 shows that the funds brought into China by the World Bank, the Asian Development Bank and other international financial institutions reached US$27.351 billion in the sixth, seventh, eighth and ninth five-year plan periods, making up 5.34% of the total foreign capital inflow or 0.3% of the GDP.

Table 4.1 Foreign investment and foreign borrowings during different periods of time

unit: US$ in 100 million

Period	1981 – 1985	1986 – 1990	1991 – 1995	1996 – 2000	Total
Total foreign investment	151.07	462.83	1,610.62	2,897.84	5,122.36
Foreign borrowing	97.91	301.26	455.82	559.02	1,414.01
Loans from foreign governments	27.86	74.90	125.90	132.89	361.55
Loans from IFIs	11.74	53.30	91.13	117.34	273.51
IFI loans in total foreign investment (%)	7.77	11.52	5.66	4.05	5.34
IFI in GDP (%)	0.08	0.30	0.33	0.22	
FDI	45.63	142.62	1,141.80	2,134.80	3,465.00
FDI in total foreign investment (%)	30.20	30.81	70.89	73.67	67.64
Other foreign investments	7.53	18.97	13.04	204.03	243.57
Per capita annual GDP growth (%)	9.26	6.26	10.68	7.24	8.40

Source: *China Foreign Economic Relations and Trade Yearbook* for all years.

Over the past more than 20 years, most of the IFI loans were used in projects that have a long investment period, remarkable social benefits and strategic and long-term impact on the economy of China, such as agricultural and rural development, infrastructure projects, education, health, environmental protection and poverty relief, which are areas where foreign private investors are reluctant to put their money in.

The assistance loans provided by international financial institutions to China assume the following features: the biggest in total amount but small on per capita basis①. The total amount of international loans is big, but it is very low when coming to the proportion in the total investment in the country②[2] and the proportion in GDP is also very low (Table 4.1). The proportion of international assistance loans in the total foreign investment rose at first and dropped later while FDI has been rising steadily to become the main source of foreign investment (Table 4.1). This is identical with the global development trend, that is, the proportion of development assistance by multilateral development organizations and official assistance from developed countries in the total foreign investment is becoming smaller and smaller while international private capital has been rising in a scale and speed unrivaled before[3].

According to the US Global Development Center (2003), among the 74 countries each with a per capita GNI of less than US$1,435, the proportion of international assistance made up 10.8% of GDP; among the 28 countries with a per capita GNI of less than US$1,435 – US$2,975, foreign assistance made up 1.4% of GDP[4]. Relatively speaking, international assistance received by China, a low-income country, only has a relatively small proportion in GDP, but the effect of the assistance is probably the best③[5].

Experience of international development assistance shows that IFI loans are a kind of low risk financial deficit financing means. It may have a positive effect on the development of the recipient countries, but may also cause financial pressure on the government of recipient countries which leads to opposite results. For instance some countries in Africa and Latin America that have obtained a large amount of assistance loans have not achieved great development with

① Official development assistance is large in amount, but per capital amount and proportion in GDP are small for China. On the per capita basis, it was only US$2 for China, US$5 for Pakistan, US$6 for Uzbekstan, US$13 for Viet Nam, US$36 for Cambodia and US$99 for Mongolia. In terms of proportion in GDP, it was 0.2% for China and 4.1% – 26.7% for other countries. China is one of the seven low level recipient countries in accepting regional technical assistance.

② The proportion of official development assistance fund is less than 1.5% of total government spending and 0.7% in total fixed assets investment.

③ World Bank Operation Evaluation Department holds that China's projects are better than the world average and the satisfaction of a considerable number of projects has gone far beyond the world's average level. This has been further testified to by projects completed since 1980. The proportion of unsatisfactory projects made up only 9% in China while the world's average in the same period was 31%.

international assistance. The quantitative studies of the relationship between international assistance and economic growth by different scholars have not led to any unanimous conclusions. Most scholars have identified a saturation point in international assistance when international assistance rises to 15% – 45% in GDP, and beyond this, the role of international assistance would drop or reduced progressively. Some scholars hold that the broad range of the saturation point is associated with the development policies, institutional quality and reachability of development projects in different countries[6]. This shows that international development assistance cannot automatically or naturally stimulate the economic growth of recipient countries, unless these countries introduce economic reforms, adjust economic structures, open up to the outside world and practice good governance.

Over the past more than 20 years, China's per capita income has risen sharply; the number of poor population has been reduced markedly; and development capabilities have improved significantly. It has in fact become the fourth largest trading country and the second largest destination of foreign direct investment. International comparison shows that the proportion of IFI loans made up only a small part of GDP, less than 0.5%. There is no country in the world with such a low income and such a low proportion of international assistance that has been so successful in development. Is their a certain relationship between these development achievements and IFI loans? What impact have IFI loans had on China's economic growth, investment and social development? How to carry out a quantitative study that covers different periods of time, different regions and different sectors? As there is a big regional disparity in the development in China, what impact do the IFI assistance loans have on different regions? Has this impact helped enlarge or narrow the regional disparities? Up to the present, no quantitative analysis as such has been carried out by any Chinese or foreign researchers.

Entrusted by the International Department of the Ministry of Finance, the authors of this paper have made a systematic, historical and objective evaluation of IFI assistance loans over the past two decades. The paper is the part on macro evaluation of this study. We shall publish the other parts soon.

4.1.2 Methods, Contents and Data Sources of the Study

According to general definition, loans by international financial institutions belong to assistance loans. In recent scores of years, the studies on different categories of loans have become an independent area of study that has its own particular method of research, known as assistance loan evaluation method, chiefly, the single equation evaluation econometric model. It was put forward in the 1960s and became nearly perfect by the 1990s. Usually, the dependent variable is economic growth rate and independent variables are the proportion of the amount of assistance, domestic bank savings and other funds in GDP; the equation also includes various control variables. This area of study has developed by leaps and bounds in the recent dozen years.

The main targets of evaluation are divided into two major categories: the impact of assistance loans on the economic growth of recipient countries; and the substitutability of assistance loans. We have evaluated IFI loans in line with these two categories, such as substitutability of domestic savings and substitutability of domestic and foreign private investment.

We have made the evaluation at two different levels: state level and provincial level. Data for computation come from China Statistical Yearbook for all years and statistical yearbooks for 31 provinces, autonomous regions and municipalities under the direct administration of the central government, the China Foreign Economic Relations and Trade Yearbook, the China Foreign Economic Relations Statistical Yearbook and the International Economic Statistical Yearbook of all issues. The data cover the period of 1978 – 2001.

Chapter listed the results of the computation: (1) single equation growth model, both national and provincial, with the subdivision of models on the eastern, middle and western regions (see Table 9.17); (2) simultaneous equation growth model, which calculates the immediate and mid-term impact of IFI loans (see Table 9.18); the model on the impact of IFI loans on bank savings (see Table 9.19); the model on the impact of IFI loans on FDI (see Table 9.20), the model of the impact of IFIs on the liquidity of the state (see Table 9.21); the model of the impact of IFI loans on regional liquidity (see Table 9.22); and the equation of the liquidity of IFI loans in the eastern, middle and western parts of the country (see Tables 9.23 and 9.24).

4.1.3 Preliminary Conclusions of the Study

During the inflow of IFI loans, China gained a high speed growth and succeeded in transition of the economic system, including financial and taxation systems, thus developed into an open society with a big inflow of FDI from a closed-door economy. During this period, the IFI loans had its impact on many aspects of China's development. IFI loans had a strong inducement effect on economic growth and the inflow private capital and international private capital. They played a supporting role in transition of the public investment system and government spending. They have also played a balancing role in easing the conflict of regional disparities, evening out the competitiveness of different regions, effectively stimulating the economic growth in less-developed areas and in narrowing the gaps between the middle and western parts of the country. Objectively speaking, IFI loans have had a positive impact on and made major contributions to China's economic development.

4.1.3.1 IFI Loans Stimulated China's Economic Growth after the 1990s

Calculation results show (see Table 4.1) that IFI loans did little to stimulate economic growth before the 1990s and they played a positive role in stimulating economic growth after that. During the 1980s, IFI loans increased at an annual rate of 1% and its contribution to economic growth was −14.1%. But after the 1990s, a 1% growth a year brought about a 5.5% economic growth.

There are a few possible reasons for this. First, the IFI loans in the early 1980s were small in amount, with its proportion in GDP being very low, about 0.06% during the sixth five-year plan period. In the late 1980s, IFI loans began to increase, accounting for about 0.30% of GDP. Up to the 1990s, the IFI loans grew significantly, with its proportion in GDP reaching 0.33% in the eighth five-year plan period and 0.22% during the ninth five-year plan period.

Second, IFIs overhauled their loan strategy to China in the 1990s. According to the environmental adaptation and learning curve, the quality of loans in the 1990s was better than that in the 1980s.

Third, China enhanced its independence in economic growth, complementary to IFI loans. Despite the fact that the IFI loans were small in terms of its proportion in GDP, their roles of pushing China's economic growth was significant.

4.1.3.2 IFI Loans Stimulated Economic Growth in Less-Developed Regions

In terms of regions, IFI loans promoted the economic growth in the 1990s. The middle and western parts of the country were the main beneficiaries. IFI loans did not have much influence on the eastern part (see Table 9.17 in Appendix of Chapter 9).

IFI loans had a significant impact on economic growth in the western part of the country. Such loans flowing to that part of the country increased at an annual rate of 1%, contributing to 4.45% of the economic growth. This shows that IFI loans are highly efficient in pulling the economic growth in that part of the country. In the middle part of the country, the economic growth was raised by about 1.3% for every 1% of IFI loans flowing to the middle part of the country. Comparing the eastern and western parts, data for the middle part are the most complete and the most representative provinces were selected and, therefore, the calculation results are the most reliable. In the eastern part, the economic growth dropped by 4% for every 1% additional IFI loans. This conclusion is drawn on the basis of the data for the 1990s. This shows that the marginal contribution by IFI loans is no longer significant and the economic development in the eastern part is no longer at the investment-pulled growth period.

What shown above is that IFI loans have different roles in stimulating economic growth in different regions, because different regions vary greatly in investment composition. In the 1990s, the proportion of FDI and private investment were high in the eastern region while the proportion of IFI loans was low. But in the middle and western regions, the proportion of FDI and private investment was relatively low while IFI loans were relatively high. Then, the IFI loans began to change the direction of their flow in the 1990s, shifting from the eastern region to the middle and western regions. Loan investment in the eastern part dropped while that in the middle and western parts rose significantly. This shows that IFIs moved to keep pace with the regional development strategy of the Chinese government and reoriented their loans toward the same direction as Chinese government did.

4.1.3.3 IFI Loans are Instrumental to Stimulating Long-Term Economic Growth

The objectives of IFI loans are usually long-term sustainable economic growth and social development and we should study their contributions to economic growth along this direction.

For instance, the purpose and primary strategy of the World Bank is to stimulate long-term economic development and reduce poverty, such as in agriculture, rural development, infrastructure construction, education, health and environmental protection as well as energy and urban utility development. This is a kind of public investment or quasi-public investment. IFI loans are mainly used to invest in public areas such as the development of energy sources, communications and urban construction and, through improving investment environment, attract the inflow of private capital to pull the economic growth. Their impact is gradual and of mid- and long-term.

The econometric analysis results show that, for every 1% of IFI loans flowing in, the cumulative average contribution to economic growth in the ensuing five years is 8.39% (see attached Table 9.18).

For every 1% additional inflow of IFI loans, the cumulative private investment would increase by 14.88% and the total investment would increase by 2.2%. The multiplication effect of IFI loans is very significant.

Apart from helping improve the investment environment in order to attract more foreign capital, IFI loans have a substituting effect on public investment. For every 1% additional inflow of loans, the public investment would be reduced by 12.67%. It is by raising the efficiency of public investment to help with the transition of public investment and eliminate the distorted allocation of social resources, thus stimulating the economic growth.

4.1.3.4 IFI Loans have Stimulated Long-Term Growth of Private Investment

For a developing country or region, one of the major objectives to use IFI assistance loans is to develop a "blood creation" mechanism rather than "blood transfusion" mechanism. The utilization of the loans is aimed at improving the investment environment, accelerating the accumulation of private capital, attracting more private capital, thus giving birth to an economic mechanism for sustainable development. This objective of IFI loans to China has been realized.

The econometric analysis shows (just as indicated in Table 9.18 attached) that, for every 1% additional inflow of IFI loans, the amount of private investment in the following five years would increase by 14.88% and total investment would increase by 2.2%. If expressed in absolute terms, for every one yuan of IFI loans added, the private investment in the following five years would increased by 2.04 yuan. This shows that China is very successful in utilizing international assistance loans to attract private investment.

Private investment has already become the main engine of growth in China. There are many ways of using IFI loans to attract private investment: (1) to boost the confidence of investors by creating a good investment environment; (2) to pull private investment by the demonstrative effect and consumption effect of loan projects; (3) to attract private investment by enhancing the capabilities of the governments at all levels to mobilize resources and implement more policies favorable for private investment. Not only so, the process may be one of self-improvement and accumulation and IFI loans may play a role of "pulling the trigger" so that private investment would flow in incessantly and a sustainable growth would be realized.

4.1.3.5 IFI Loans have Helped Raise the Domestic Saving Level in the Eastern Part of the Country

Compared with other developing countries or regions, the domestic saving levels (percentage of domestic savings in GDP) in the eastern, middle and western parts of China are all in the front ranks. But the average level in the eastern part is nearly 10 percentage points higher than that in the middle part and nearly 20 percentage points higher than that in the western part. However, the average level of loans (percentage of loans in GDP) used in the eastern part is only 0.005% higher than that in the middle part and 0.023% higher than that in the western part. The total savings and the growth of savings in the eastern part are far more and higher than those in the middle and western parts and the inflow of foreign capital would play a catalyst role.

Econometric analysis shows (see Table 9.19 attached) that for every 1% additional IFI loans, the domestic saving level raised by 3.05% in the eastern part. But they did not have any impact in the middle and western parts and even had some negative impact. This shows that the IFI loans used in the eastern part is too small to directly pull economic growth (see the second conclusion), but they may stimulate the growth of savings, thus having an indirect pull to the economic growth.

4.1.3.6 IFI Loans have Stimulated the FDI to Flow into the Eastern Part

The econometric analysis shows that IFIs has a very positive contribution to FDI inflow (see Table 9.20 attached), especially in the eastern part. For every one yuan of IFI loans added on the per capita basis, the per capita FDI attracted in the year increased by 4.8 yuan and increased by 1.8 yuan in the following year, far above the average level. But IFI loans do not have any impact in stimulating FDI inflow in the middle and western parts. In terms of attracting FDI, IFI loans are more efficient in economically developed regions. Why so?

The factors affecting the policy decision of FDI are more complicated than domestic private investment. The FDI decisions are influenced by encouragement policies, local GDP aggregate and growth, degree of opening up, the level of infrastructure facilities, local labor price and cultural similarity. IFIs has a positive impact on FDI inflow in two aspects. One is to provide infrastructure facilities and educational resources and create a good investment environment, thus serving as a catalyst for the inflow of international private capital. IFI loans per se have a certain symbolic significance. It means that the policies of the local government have been accepted by international organizations, thus improving the attractive power of the local investment.

Just as pointed out by some scholars, such as Burnside and Dollar (2000), Svensson (1999) and Dollar and Easterly (1999), capital is a major factor that affects economic growth and social development, but whether the multilateral or bilateral loans can achieve the anticipated role is determined by whether the country or region has good policies and institutional guarantee.

The eastern region has always been better than the middle and western regions in terms of economic development level and investment environment. If we say that the scale or proportion of IFI loans may symbolize the quality of the environment for private investment of a region, the eastern part of the country is obviously superior to that in the middle and western parts of the country.

4.1.4 Much Remains to be Done for More Efficiently Using IFI Loans

Over the past 20 years, IFI loans have made positive and useful contributions to China's economic transition, the transition of the financial system and even regional development. The World Bank and the Asian Development Bank have not only provided China with a large amount of capital and introduced financing from other countries and brought in advanced and practical technologies and advanced management methods common in the world into China.

The success of China in utilizing IFI loans shows:

First, it is hard to change the backwardness of economic development of a country, which is the initial historical condition and the starting point of development. But the strategic option of opening to the outside world is the basic condition and basic way to change the economic backwardness. The utilization of IFI loans is an important short-cut for opening up a low-risk, big-return investment with a strong externality. It is also an important window to link up with international economy.

Second, international assistance cannot stimulate the development of economically backward countries automatically. It is up to the recipient country to introduce structural reforms, maintain the stability of macroeconomy, provide the people with long-term service, develop human resources, constantly improve the investment environment, set store by institutional and legal system construction, strengthen capability building and establish a "blood creation" mechanism. Otherwise, development assistance is nothing but a "blood transfusion" machine.

Third, IFIs and recipient countries have established good partnership with mutual trust and mutual benefit. For instance, the Chinese government has done an excellent job in performing loan obligations and raising the efficiency of the utilization of loans. The good relations of cooperation between China and the World Bank and the Asian Development Bank can be held up as a good model and a vivid example in theoretical innovation.

Fourth, the important objective and role of international assistance are to effectively absorb international and domestic private capital so as to facilitate the sustainable development and economic transition of the recipient countries. Although time is still very short for China to use IFI loans, and more funds and knowledge are still needed from the World Bank and the Asian Development Bank in its long journey against poverty in the new century. In order to better utilize loans and bring their development efficiency to the full, the government, such as the loan project manager and loan receiver, still has much to do for further improvement.

(1) It is entirely necessary and efficient to make an even large strategic shift to the middle and western parts of the country. The middle and western parts of the country still need investment to pull their economic growth. The resources mobilization capabilities of these parts of the country are far weaker than the eastern part. It is, therefore, necessary to use public capital inflow to make up for the shortages of private capital. As the marginal effect of output in the eastern part has dropped markedly, even lower than in the middle and western parts (as shown in Table 9.7 attached), continued bias toward the eastern part is in general low efficient.

(2) It is necessary to make more investment in the infrastructure of the middle and western parts of the country. The inducement of IFI loans to FDI in the middle and western parts is weaker than that in the eastern part (see Table 9.20 attached) in that the infrastructure facilities, economic foundation and policy environment need improvements. In the middle and western parts, loan projects are mainly distributed in agriculture, health, education and environment, where capabilities of providing matching capital are weak, the period of investment recovery is long, loan projects are mostly non-productive undertakings and the capabilities of improving the local investment environment are relatively weak. While IFI loans continue to flow into these departments, it is necessary to invest more in infrastructure areas, such as communications, energy and water resources

in order to attract more international private capital.

(3) It is necessary to encourage the middle and western parts to adopt some tax reduction policies in using IFI loans and restrict such policies in the eastern part. The range of tax reduction is less in the middle and western parts than in the eastern part, but their attractiveness to private capital is larger than that in the eastern part (see Tables 9.23 and 9.24). This shows that the middle and western parts may adopt some tax reduction policies in getting loans and the eastern part should control the range of tax cuts.

(4) Loans given to provinces should match the restrictions on government spending. Although IFI loans did induce the rise in the government expenditure in the past and did not affect the growth of investment and economy (see Tables 9.21 – 9.24), this is only temporary and a compromised way to choose which is less harmful. It would inevitably cause tremendous pressure on the finance in the long run and harm economic growth and social development. In the future, prior to approving IFI loans, we should demand governments applying for loans to make institutional reforms, streamline the government, cut government spending and even lower the growth level of government spending.

(5) It is necessary to study the relations between IFI loans and the public investment structure of various provinces. The transition of public investment has been completed after 20 years of reform. The supplementary role of IFI loans in the transition of public investment should be changed into that of stimulating public investment. In the past, public investment needed to withdraw from certain areas, and on the other hand, the drawing capacity of the central finance dropped, while the government spending rose, thus being unable to sustain the resources necessary to transition, therefore, IFI loans played a role of substituting public investment in certain areas. In the future, IFI loans should play a role of stimulating public investment in health, education, social security and environmental protection instead of substituting for public investment in these areas, especially in the eastern part. Of course, as the middle and western parts still lack enough fund sources, more IFI loans should be devoted to road construction and energy development and other semi-public departments.

(6) There should be different requirements for the public investment levels of local governments with regard to public and non-public departments. In purely public departments, such as education, environmental protection, public health and rural water supply, local governments should be required to raise their public investment when using IFI loans; in semi-public departments and non-public departments, such as energy and communications, there should not be such a restriction on IFI loan projects, but the projects should be limited to the less-developed middle and western parts of the country. It is necessary to reduce IFI loans input into semi-public and non-public departments in the eastern part of the country.

(7) It is necessary to intensify information service level of governments at all levels and reduce trading cost. In the period of loan inflow, although public

investment is reduced, private capital fails to grow simultaneously as loans due to lack of information and restrictions in trading cost. There is still a lag period limiting the pulling effect of IFI loans (see Table 9.21). It is, therefore, necessary for governments at all levels to provide more information, enhance transparency and remove all restrictions on private investment.

(8) The unfavorable effect of IFI loans on export merits attention. For every 1% of additional loan inflow, export would be reduced by 0.11% (see Table 9.22). But as loan inflow brings about directly the corresponding inflow of foreign exchange, it reduces the efforts by various regions to strengthen export, which causes harmful effect on the export abilities of the backward areas in the long run and is unfavorable for the development of the middle and western regions. It is, therefore, necessary to intensify export requirements while dispensing loans.

(9) It is necessary to restrict the excessive capital goods import resulting from IFI loans. For every 1% of additional loan inflow, capital goods import would increase by 0.52% (see Table 9.21). Proper import of capital goods is favorable for improving the level of capital equipment in the region, but the preconditions should be that the import of such equipment and instruments must conform to the cost effective principle both technically and economically. For many loan projects, advanced equipment and instruments are often lying idle and causing great waste. It is, therefore, necessary to make localized revision of the principles for equipment procurement.

4.2 Microscopic Economic Evaluation

4.2.1 Indictor Design and Computation

The economic evaluation of loan projects is made up of three parts: economic performance level, loan repayment ability and impact on economic development.

Comparable performance indicators usually include financial internal return rate (FIRR), financial benefit-cost ratio (FBCR), economic international return rate (EIRR) and economic benefit-cost ratio (EBCR). We have selected FIRR and EIRR as the weighing indicators and EIRR as a contrast indicator according to the collection of data from project survey.

In converting FIRR, we have established that the projects two time higher than the benchmark return rate are rated as highly successful or HS and those 1 – 2 times higher than the benchmark returns are rated as successful or S and those lower than the benchmark returns but half higher than the benchmark returns are rated as unsuccessful or U, and those half lower than the benchmark returns as highly unacceptable or HU. In the conversion of FBRC, those two times higher are rated as HS, those 1 – 2 times higher are rated as S, those 0.5 – 1 times higher as U and those lower than 0.5 are rated as HU.

The comparable performance indicator is the average value of FIRR and FBCR. In the process of addition, HS, S, U, and HU are 1.00, 0.75, 0.50 and 0.25, respectively. If the average value is between 0.75 – 1.00, the comparable performance indicator is HS; when it is between 0.50 – 0.75, the comparable performance indicator is S. If the average value is between 0.25 – 0.50, the indicator is U; if the average value is between 0 – 0.25, the indicator is HU. Loan repayment ability and impact on economic development are, too, divided into four grades: HS, S, U and HU. Loan repayment ability can also be divided into "totally capable of loan repayment", "partially capable of loan repayment", "poor capability of loan repayment" and "totally incapable of loan repayment". The indicators of impact on economic development are divided into four grades: significant, general, poor and no impact.

The end result of economic evaluation is the mean value of the three indictors of economic performance level, loan repayment ability and impact on economic development. The method of computation is the same as the synthesization of economic performance indicators. The indicators are shown in Table 4.2.

Table 4.2 Economic efficient evaluation indicators and grading

Indicator	HS	S	U
FIRR	More than one time higher than benchmark returns	1 – 2 times higher than the benchmark returns	Lower than the benchmark returns
FBCR	More than 2 times higher than benefit-cost	1 – 2 times higher than the benefit-cost	Benefit-cost lower than 1

4.2.2 Results of Evaluation

In general, of the 32 sample projects, 11 are rated as HS, accounting for 34.4%, 11 are rated as S, accounting for 34.4% and 9 are rated as U, accounting for 28.1% and one is rated as UA, accounting for 3.1% (see Fig. 4.1). Projects that are generally successful make up over two-thirds (68.8%). This shows that most of the IFI loan projects are very successful economically and have achieved good economic results. What merits attention is that unsuccessful and unacceptable projects make up nearly one-third (31.2%), far higher than the total figure of IFI loan projects. This is because a considerable part of IFI loan projects has development functions and capability building orientation, quite different from projects that seek economic efficiency only. Its specialty is reflected in the comprehensive economic and social environment efficiency. It is, therefore, not very satisfactory to evaluate it purely from economic angle.

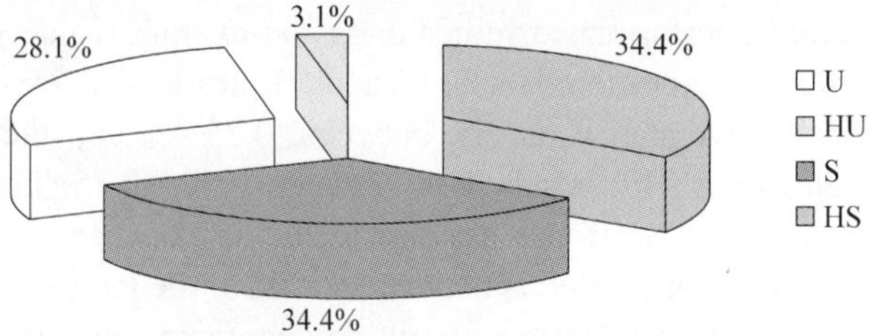

Figure 4.1 Proportions of various grades of economic evaluation

In terms of various sectors, the economic efficiency of such large infrastructure projects as energy and communications is in general good and the number of projects above the successful grade makes up 75% and 83.3% (see Table 4.3). The economic efficiency of purely competitive projects and purely public welfare projects as education and health is relatively poor and the number of projects rated as unsuccessful and unacceptable makes up 50% (see Table 4.3). The economic efficiency of mixed projects such as agriculture, water supply and environmental protection is of middle grade, which is inseparable from the orientation and characteristics of IFI loans.

Table 4.3 Number and percentage of various grades of economic evaluation

	HS		S		U		HU	
	Number	%	Number	%	Number	%	Number	%
Agriculture	3	33.3	3	33.3	2	22.2	1	11.1
Industry	1	50.0			1	50.0		
Energy	2	50.0	1	25.0	1	25.0		
Communications	3	50.0	2	33.3	1	16.7		
Education			1	50.0	1	50.0		
Health			2	50.0	2	50.0		
Water supply and environmental health	1	50.0	1	50.0				
Urban construction					1	100.0		
Environmental protection	1	50.0	1	50.0				
Total	11	34.4	11	34.4	9	28.1	1	3.1

In terms of region, there are more successful projects in the eastern part, with the proportion reaching 95.3%, far higher than in the middle and western parts. Although the number of highly successful projects is 7.1% more than in the western part, the number of projects above the successful grade is 21.2% less than in the western part. This is directly associated with the project distribution. But it mainly reflects the capabilities of implementing projects and the abilities of organizations. The economically developed eastern part has developed a favorable cycle in using loans and this should be the orientation the middle and western parts should work for Fig. 4.2.

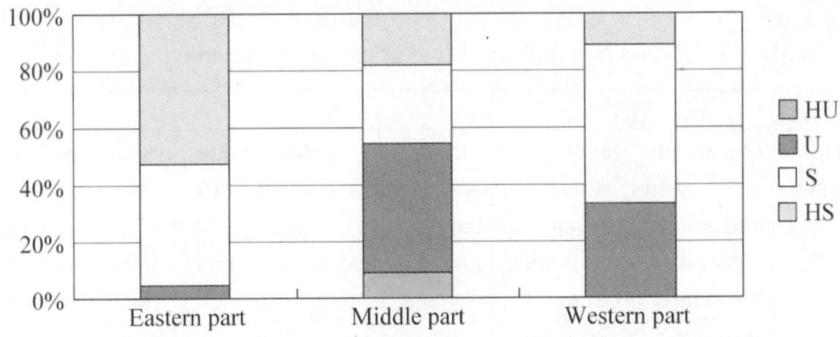

Figure 4.2 Regional differences in economic evaluation

4.3 Environment Evaluation

4.3.1 Indicator Design and Computation

Environment evaluation of loan projects is divided into two parts: comparable environment indicators and comparable ecological indicators.

Comparable environment indicators usually include waste water discharge level, waste gas discharge level, solid waste discharge level and noise level. The four indicators can be divided into four grades: HS, S, U and HU. The discharge levels of waste water, waste gas and solid waste can be divided into weakening discharge intensity, maintaining discharge intensity, increasing discharge intensity and seriously increasing discharge intensity. Noise level indicators can be graded as totally no impact, weak impact, middle-degree impact and significant impact.

The comparable environment indicator is the mean value of the waste water discharge level, waste gas discharge level, solid waste discharge level and noise level. In the process of addition, HS is 1.00, S is 0.75, U is 0.50, and HU is 0.25. When the mean value is 0.75 – 1.00, the comparable environment indicator is HS; when the value is 0.50 – 0.75, the indicator is S; when the value is 0.25 – 0.50, the indicator is U; when the value is 0 – 0.25, the indicator is HU.

Comparable ecological indicators usually include water and soil conservation ability and impact on biodiversity. The two indicators are also divided into four grades: HS, S, U and HU. The waster and soil conservation ability can be graded as fairly strong, strong, poor and incapable. The indicators on the biodiversity impact are divided into four grades: stimulating impact, no impact, unfavorable impact and significantly unfavorable impact. The comparable ecological indicator composition is the same as comparable environmental indicators.

The end ecological environmental evaluation is the mean value of comparable environment indicators and comparable ecological indicators, and the method of computation is the same as the composition method of comparable environmental indicators as shown below in Table 4.4.

Table 4.4 Evaluation indicators and grades of environmental efficiency

Indicator	HS	S	U
Comparable environment indicators	Discharge levels of waste water, waste gas and solid waste can be weakened and noise has totally no impact	Levels of waste water, waste gas and solid waste belong to maintainable intensity and noise impact is weak	Levels of waste water, waste gas and solid waste belong to increasing discharge intensity and noise has certain impact
Comparable ecological indictors	With fairly strong water and soil conservation ability and a stimulating role in biodiversity	With a certain degree of water and soil conservation ability and no role in stimulating biodiversity	With poor or totally no ability of water and soil conservation and un-favorable impact on biodiversity

4.3.2 Results of Evaluation

Of the 26 sample projects, nine are rated as HS, accounting for 34.6%; 14 are rated as S, accounting for 53.8%; three are rated as U, accounting for 11.6% (see Fig. 4.3). The general success rate is 88.4%. This shows that the overwhelming majority of IFI loan projects are very successful in the ecological area and keep pace with the general strategic objectives of sustainable development. What merits attention is that the unsuccessful projects and failure projects in the economic evaluation are basically identical with the general unsuccessful and failure projects evaluated by IFIs. This is mainly because the IFI loan strategy has clear orientation toward sustainable development and that is why the general evaluation is identical with ecological environment evaluation.

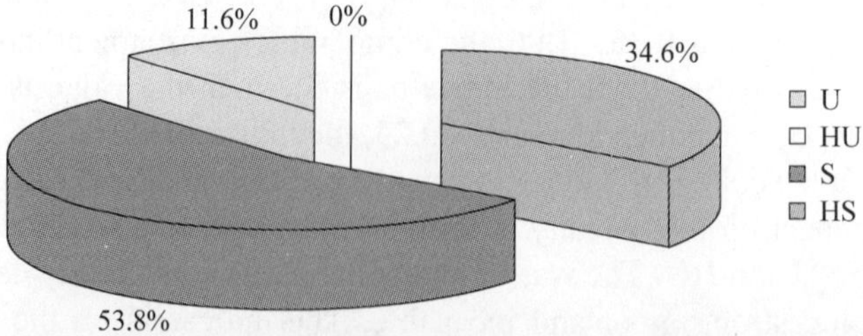

Figure 4.3 Percentage of various grades in ecological evaluation

As seen from projects in various sectors, the ecological environment efficiency is generally good in environmental protection and agriculture and other comprehensive projects, with a success rate of more than 90% (see Table 4.5). Projects in energy and industry and other traditional polluting areas also realized good ecological efficiency thanks to the strict requirements by IFIs (see Table 4.5). But the evaluation is low in communications projects due to common noise problems, with unsuccessful projects accounting for two-thirds.

Table 4.5 Number and percentage of grades in sector-specific ecological evaluation

	HS		S		U		HU	
	Number	%	Number	%	Number	%	Number	%
Agriculture	3	33.3	5	55.6	1	11.1		
Industry	1	50.0	1	50.0				
Energy	2	50.0	2	50.0				
Communications			4	66.7	2	33.3		
Water supply and environmental health	1	50.0	1	50.0				
Urban construction			1	100.0				
Environmental protection	2	100.0						
Water supply and environmental health								
Total	9	34.6	14	53.8	3	11.6		

As can be seen from the ecological evaluation of projects in different parts of the country, economic development and ecological environment are better coordinated in the western part of the country, thanks to the guidance of the new approach to development, with all projects reaching the successful grade. As the eastern part began to pay attention to ecology after a very long period of economic development, the middle part is still in the extensive development stage and pay much attention to economic, efficiency, therefore, nearly 20% of the projects subject to ecological evaluation are not successful (see Fig. 4.4). This is a problem that merits attention in future development.

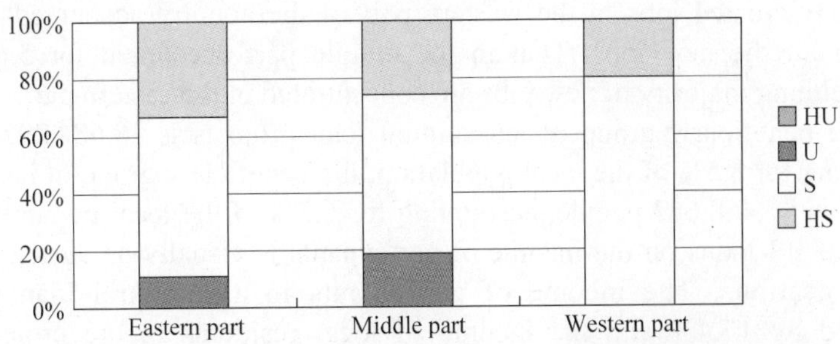

Figure 4.4 Composition of regional ecological evaluation indicators

4.4 Social Impact Evaluation

IFI loans to China are mostly used in important areas such as agriculture, environmental protection and health that concern the national economic development and the people's livelihood. They have brought about tremendous economic results and also had far-reaching social benefits. This manifests itself in creating more jobs, increasing the income of local residents, promoting reform of public policies and raising the transfer payments of local finances. The evaluation of the social impact of the World Bank and Asian Development Bank loan projects in China is to see whether they are successful, meanwhile, this is an important aspect for studying the efficiency of use of the funds.

4.4.1 Evaluation Indicator System

Loan projects in different areas have different social impact. In selecting evaluation indicators, we have biased toward different areas and the data collection and evaluation methods are also different. In the light of the characteristics of 39 sample projects, the evaluation indicators mainly cover impact on human resources, impact on public policies, project research achievements and application of information technology. We adopted numerical value data as the basis for evaluation and adopted descriptive data for other indicators (see Table 4.6).

4.4.2 Evaluation Results

4.4.2.1 Impact on Human Resources

Of the sample projects, agricultural projects have a big pulling effect on employment, with the employment population increasing by 1,758,309 people. For every US$327 of loans from the World Bank and the Asian Development Bank, there is an additional job created. But the distribution is not even enough. The newly created jobs in the western part of the country accounted for only 2.7% of all the new jobs. That in the middle part accounted for 5.6%. The overwhelming majority of new jobs are concentrated in the eastern part.

The beneficiary group of agricultural loan projects is 18,684,297 people, accounting for 8.5% of the local population; the beneficiary group of health loan projects is 87,468,662 people, accounting for 6.7% of the local population. The impact of IFI loans on the income of participants is visually on agriculture and communications. The income of participants in agricultural loan projects increased by 17.4% and the income of local residents in the project areas increased by 7.1%, higher than the per capita net income growth of 5% in the

Table 4.6 Social impact evaluation indicator system

Indicator	HS	S	U
Pull to employment	Increasing jobs, basically meeting the percentages set at the time of project proposal	Increasing jobs, covering a certain scope of beneficiaries	Bringing about employment growth to a certain degree but beneficiaries are not identical with that in the project proposal
Changes in the income of participants in projects	Project participants receive corresponding management and technical training and their incomes change significantly	Project participants receive training and their income rise markedly as compared with non-project participants	Training is not put in place or income does not change much
Impact on public services	Projects change local government's institutional arrangements and management methods and change transfer payments correspondingly	There are no changes in government institutional arrangements and management or project did not have any impact on local government's transfer payments	Projects did not have any impact on institutional arrangements and management and local government's transfer payments do not change with the projects
Social motivation effect	Projects can attract more private capital to take an active part in the areas and have obvious social motivation effect	Projects can attract private capital and have certain social motivation effect	Project cannot attract private capital and the social demonstrative effect is poor

same period. The income of participants in communications loan projects increased by 9.2% and the income of local residents in the project areas increased by 7.7%, higher than the per capita net income growth of 5% in the same period. Agricultural and health loan projects organized more than 76,000 training courses, with 1,573,000 trainees.

This shows that the World Bank and the Asian Development Bank loan projects in China have had marked impact on human resources of project participants and local residents, especially in agriculture, health and communications areas, where such impact is more obvious. This has not only helped improving the living standards of the local residents but also improve the qualities of the labor force, thus accumulating human capital for the sustainable development of the projects. But one thing that cannot be ignored is that the impact is not at the same level between urban and rural areas, and among different parts of the country, thus resulting in an irrational distribution of the active roles. The future loan projects should be more biased toward the western part of the country.

4.4.2.2 Impact on Public Policies

Loan projects in different sectors have different impacts on local policies. 56% of agricultural projects, 19% of water supply and environmental projects, 13% of energy and health projects have affected local policies, directly stimulating the introduction of new institutional arrangements or management methods. But industrial projects and education projects have little or no impact on local policies at all. Loan projects in different sectors have different impacts on local finances. Of the projects that affected local finances, agricultural projects accounted for 44%, energy, water supply and environmental projects accounted for 19% and communications and health projects accounted for 6%. They contributed directly to local finances. Industrial and education projects had little or no impact on local finances at all. Private capital participation was poor. Only 25% of the agricultural projects and 6% of communication projects had the participation of private capital. Projects in other sectors had no private capital participation. Agricultural loan projects, about 69%, had obvious social motivation effect. 6% of projects in industry, communications, education and health displayed such roles. But such roles of the projects in energy, water supply and environment are not so obvious (see Fig. 4.5).

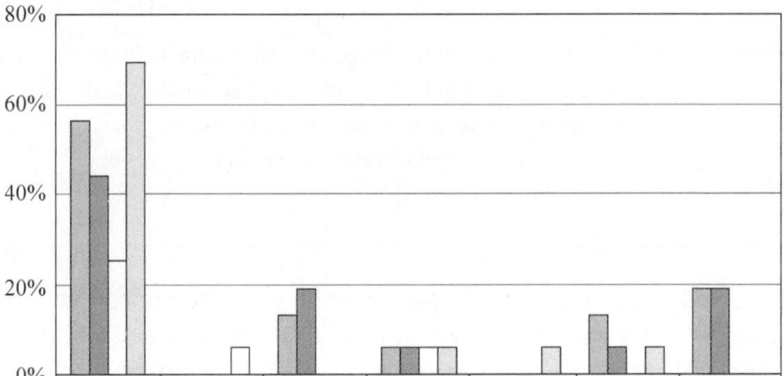

	Agriculture	Industry	Energy	Communi-cation	Education	Health	Water supply environment
Impact on policty	56%	0%	13%	6%	0%	13%	19%
Impact on finance	44%	0%	19%	6%	0%	6%	19%
Private investment	25%	0%	0%	6%	0%	0%	0%
Motivation effect	69%	6%	0%	6%	6%	6%	0%

Figure 4.5 Percentage of public indicators in different sectors

This shows that in all sectors, agricultural projects had the biggest public impact, demonstrating a very high sensitivity of agriculture to funds and policy. In industry and education, however, the public impact is confined to social mobilization effect brought about by projects themselves, but their impact on public services is meager. The indicators of public impact show that participation of private capital is usually very low in sectors other than agriculture, reflecting the ignorance of the roles of private capital in utilizing foreign investment. It is, therefore, necessary to further promote matching reforms of political structure, optimization of the public service functions of the government and formulate policies for encouraging private capital to participate in large projects.

4.4.2.3 Research Achievements of Projects

Of all the sample projects, only 7.7% are rated good in research achievements and 20.5% are rated poor. Among the good projects, two-thirds are education projects. This indicates that only a small proportion of IFI loan projects yielded research achievements, demonstrating the stress on physical construction and the neglect of research, a phenomenon that is unfavorable for the technical overflow of projects, therefore, it weakens, to a certain extent, the utilization rate of loans. In the future, efforts should be made to intensify the sense of research achievements and promote their application.

4.4.2.4 Application of Information Technology

The application of information technology in loan projects reflects the impact on promotion of the projects. Owing to the widespread of network information technology, the utilization of these technologies cannot only improve the efficiency of project implementation but also facilitate the expansion of influence of projects through information and achievements sharing. Of the sample projects, 10.3% developed special computer application systems and 12.8% popularized the use of computers. Other projects still stayed at hand-operation and simple computer application stage.

4.5 Evaluation of Sustainability

Over 80% of the loans provided by the World Bank and the Asian Development Bank are used to develop infrastructure facilities and it is, therefore, necessary to ensure good sustainability so that they would display their roles in a considerably long period of time to come, thus realizing the maximization of loan effect.

4.5.1 Evaluation Indicator System

Many factors are involved with respect to the sustainability of loan projects, and its evaluation should be carried out with comprehensive analysis according to many indicators. The normal continuity of projects may be regarded as the ability of self operation without financial and technical support from external financial institutions after the close of loan projects, and the sustainability and high quality of the output of projects. The evaluation of the sustainability of loan projects may start from two kinds of indicators. One kind are the static indicators that reflect whether or not the projects have attained the anticipated objectives in the feasibility study reports after its completion and the contents of evaluation of the self survival ability by lenders, which serve as the basis for further development of the projects; the other kind are dynamic indicators, which covers the continuity of project supervision organizations, the ability of project managers to realize objectives and other indicators expressing dynamic development. The combination of the two kinds of indicators can completely draw a picture of the development trend from the completion of the projects to independent operation. The specific indicators are shown in Table 4.7.

Table 4.7 Sustainability evaluation indicator system

Indicator	HS	S	U
Current operation of projects	After project completion, project implementation units still have the intention to and ability to continue the projects and the project supervision organizations are still there	After project completion, project implementation units still have the intention and ability to continue the projects, but project supervision organizations are dissolved with the completion of projects	After project completion, project implementation units did not have the ability to continue the projects and supervision organizations disappeared
Duplicability of projects	Projects can provide good experience or lessons for similar projects, and their management system and ideas are duplicable	Projects can provide certain experience for similar projects, but part of the experience has certain special features	Project experience and lessons are independent, unable to be spread for application
Risk dealing mechanism	A good risk dealing mechanism ensures the continuity of projects after the close of bank accounts	A certain risk dealing mechanism ensures a certain financing channel for the operation of projects	A risk dealing mechanism can ensure project financing after the closure of bank accounts, and also, projects are not closed or delayed

4.5.2 Evaluation Results

4.5.2.1 Static Indicators

Of the sample projects, 15.4% are rated successful, which are mostly distributed in agricultural and health projects, with agricultural projects accounting for 83% and health projects, 17%. Other projects were not evaluated by lenders due to unknown factors. Of the projects, 41% are operating well and 35.9% are operating with the two combined accounting for 76.9%. The rest 1/4 projects underwent a shift in functions or died out. Projects in energy, health, water supply and environmental protection are all in normal operation, which are associated with good economic efficiency or small repayment pressure. Half of the industrial projects are in abnormal operation, reflecting difficulties after IFIs terminated investment (see Fig. 4.6).

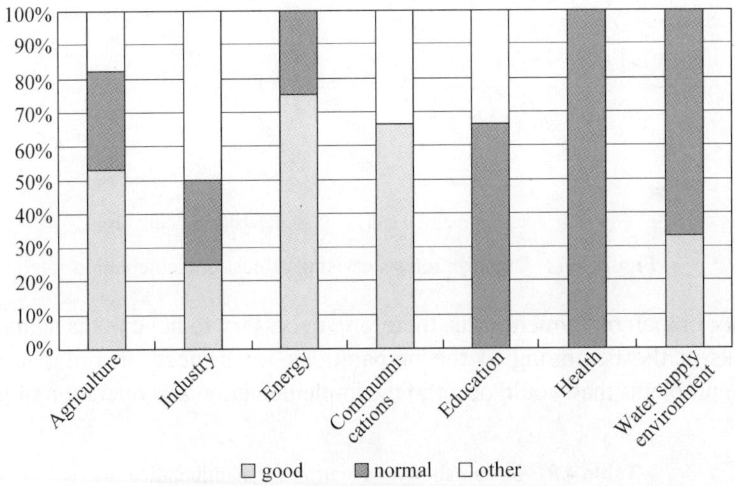

Figure 4.6 Current operation of projects

About 59% of the projects' supervision organizations still existed after the completion of the projects. Such organizations in energy project were 100% existent, reflecting the strict control of energy projects by the government. Such control in industrial projects was the weakest. It is associated with the operation of industrial projects. Part of the industrial enterprises met difficulty after losing government protection and became unable to pay back the loans.

4.5.2.2 Dynamic Indicators

Objective unanimity is the highest in energy and education projects, which is closely associated with the their nature as (para)public goods. Such affiliations all exceeded 50% in agriculture and industrial projects, reflecting the uniformity of state policies and more common experience for similar projects to borrow. The objective uniformity and duplicability are low in education projects, demonstrating that different regions and different levels of education models have big disparities and that the accelerated reform of the educational system has impact on loan projects (see Table 4.8). Only 7.7% of the projects have mechanisms for resisting risks, revealing that China's foreign investment and loan projects lack the sense of risk control and lack long-term planning and responsive mechanisms. Once there is external impact, it is likely to cause

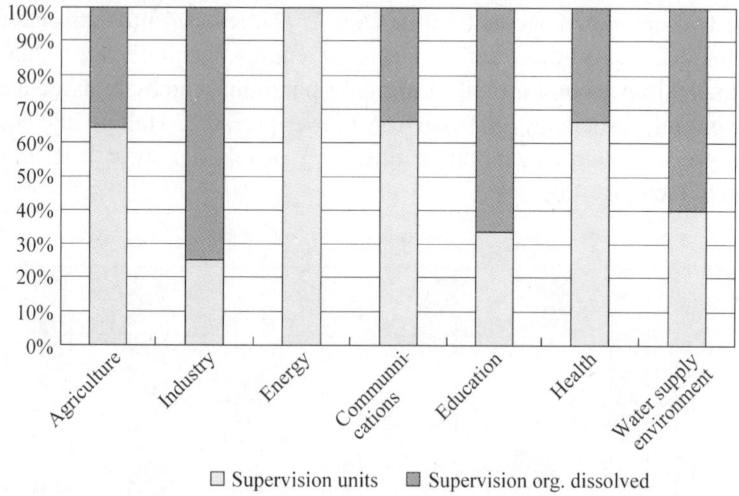

Figure 4.7 Organization supervising project implementation

difficulty in loan repayment. It is, therefore, necessary to have plans against crisis and risks at the beginning of the preparations for projects in order to prevent possible problems that would occur in the implementation and operation of projects.

Table 4.8 Sustainability evaluation's dynamic indicators

	Objective uniformity (yes)			Duplicability(yes)		
	Quantity	%		Quantity	%	
		In total	In sector		In total	In sector
Agriculture	14	35.9	82.4	9	23.1	52.9
Industry	2	5.1	50	2	5.1	50
Energy	4	10.3	100	2	5.1	50
Communication	2	5.1	66.7	1	2.6	33.3
Education	1	2.6	33.3	2	5.1	33.3
Health	3	7.7	100	2	5.1	100
Water supply and Environment	4	10.3	80	2	5.1	40

4.6 Summary and Policy Recommendations

4.6.1 Summary

In our post-project evaluation, we have carried out studies of technical assistance projects. But, owing to problems of projects per se, we have not been able to carry out detailed investigations into these projects. But in our grading, we have put technical progress and technology diffusion into the indicators about management system, IFI performance, lenders performance and social impact. They are therefore not listed separately here.

Based on the four evaluation indicator systems for the results and impact and by taking into account factors such as system building and technical progress, we may make a comprehensive evaluation of the results and impact of the projects. But in the process of grading, owing to the fact that different projects are different in corresponding indicators in terms of importance, we have given them different weighting in our comprehensive evaluation. Here, we have given different values of weights to indicators of different sectors and thus arrived at the end conclusions (Table 4.9).

Table 4.9 Sector distribution of successes of projects

	Economy	Environ-ment	Social impact	Sustaina-bility	System	Evaluation result
Agriculture	S	HS	HS	HS	HS	HS
Industry	U	S	S	U	HS	U
Energy	HS	S	S	HS	S	HS
Communication	HS	U	S	S	U	S
Education	U	S	HS	HS	HS	HS
Health	U	S	S	HS	HS	S
Water supply and environmental health	S	S	S	S	HS	S
Urban construction	S	S	S	U	HS	S
Environmental protection	S	HS	S	S	U	HS
Evaluation result	S	HS	HS	HS	HS	

Table 4.9 shows that most projects have achieved good results and social impact. On the one hand, the objectives of projects have basically been realized, helping greatly improve agriculture, infrastructure and social services. On the other hand, loan projects have brought in common international management experience, production technologies and new institutional arrangements, which have played a good, demonstrative role and provided a lot of experience for similar projects. But we have also found that, as industrial projects have strong competitive power and demand high flexibility and autonomy, they are not suitable for such kinds of assistance loans. Although such loans are needed in development, we need other financing means. That is why IFIs have cut assistance loans to industrial projects since the latter half of the 1990s.

4.6.2 Policy Recommendations

It has been more than 20 years since China implemented IFI loan projects. This has stimulated the construction of infrastructure projects and brought out direct economic results. What is more important is that these projects have had a large impact on the ideas, thoughts and capabilities of project construction, management and government management projects. In a sense, they also have a certain impact on institutional arrangements. After carrying out post project evaluation and analysis, we may accumulate a lot of experience in project management (Table 4.10) to shed light on project management in the future.

Table 4.10 Project experience and lessons and policy recommendations

	Experience and lesson	Policy recommendation
Objective evaluation		
Project objectives	1. Some objectives of project design did not conform to reality and state development strategies therefore, they have to make way for other priority projects.	1. National conditions and state development strategies should be taken into account at the time of project proposal in order to prevent duplication of projects and operation of overdue projects.
	2. Changes in external market and policy made it difficult to realize the objectives.	2. It is necessary to know the emphasis of IFI country assistance strategy and to have different ways and strength of fiscal support to different types of projects. 3. It is necessary to have the courage of rejecting projects that do not conform to market environment and policy requirements.
Process evaluation		
Institutional development effect	1. New institutional arrangements and designs introduced by most projects have a certain demonstrative effect and the experience accumulated in implementation of the projects is favorable for the implementation of other projects.	1. It is necessary to spread the application of management system and supervision mechanism that conform to Chinese conditions and standardize them.
	2. Changes in project implementation units and project management units can bring out losses in efficiency and finance.	2. It is necessary to maintain the stability of project management units and concentrate responsibilities and power that should be directly linked with financial supply and project implementation units.

Continued

	Experience and lesson	Policy recommendation
Institutional development effect		3. It is necessary to establish an effective and powerful coordination mechanism, so that departments are associated with the projects and take an active part in them. 4. It is necessary to set up the third party supervision mechanism.
Performance of IFIs	1. Low level participation by IFIs in project proposal and feasibility studies, and weak ability in project choice leads to a series of problems.	1. To standardize processes of project proposal and feasibility studies so as to prevent big gaps between project proposal and reality.
	2. Mid-term adjustment plays an important role.	2. To let project consulting companies to participate in the operation of projects, set up project data bank and provide detailed information on projects.
	3. Experts play a big supporting role in project processes and financial and technical affairs but at the same time lead to rigidity and response lag.	3. To increase transparency of the project process and weigh transparency and operational efficiency.
Performance of lenders	1. Matching funds play a big role, but general matching funds proportion is low and poor in disbursement.	1. To intensify participation of lenders.
	2. Lenders do enough to promote and publicize projects and to tie projects to local research organizations, which is a new institutional innovation.	2. To raise the awareness of repayment, enhance the project self financing capabilities and survival ability, encourage private capital to participate in and set up feasible loan repayment mechanism.
	3. The sense of loan repayment is weak and there is basically no loan repayment mechanism.	3. Government should undertake losses for policy changes and provide financial support by way of incorporating debt repayment into budget. 4. To protect the interests of private investors and prevent them from being squeezed out by government behavior, to make timely adjustment of the project objectives and operational modes to better suit the requirements of reality and to establish an innovation incentive and risk coping package.

Continued

	Experience and lesson	Policy recommendation
Impact and result evaluation		
Economic efficiency	1. Project implementation and ability to match organizations are still weak. 2. Most areas are poor in their abilities of using economic resources.	1. To strengthen supervision and management by local governments. 2. To raise the ability of using funds. 3. To introduce a third party supervision mechanism to prevent loopholes in funds.
Environmental protection efficiency	1. Project loan strategy stresses policy of environmental protection. 2. Environmental protection is directly associated with local economic development model.	1. To make environmental protection one of the objectives of the projects and foster the idea of green development. 2. To shift economic development model and stress the unity of economic growth and development.
Social benefit	1. IFI projects, especially public projects ensure the broadness of beneficiaries, but there are big gaps between urban and rural areas. 2. Social motivation effects of the projects are obvious, but their impact in public areas is limited, little on improving public services and the weak ability of promoting private involvement. 3. Projects often stress physical construction to the neglect of researches.	1. To achieve more bias toward the middle and western parts of the country in approving loan projects. 2. To carry out reform of administrative system of the government, optimize public service functions of the government and formulate policies to encourage private capital to participate. 3. To intensify achievement awareness and stimulate the application of achievements.
Sustainable development	1. Most projects establish supervision mechanisms to maintain the implementation, but these mechanisms exist in names only after the projects are closed and bank accounts are terminated. 2. Overwhelming majority of projects do not set up proper risk avoidance mechanisms and are unable to cope with changes in policy environment.	1. To prevent project from being terminated with the termination of loans through proper institutional arrangements and encourage project self financing. 2. To make risk avoidance plans at the beginning of projects so as to avoid external impact and operational risks.

References

[1] Asian Development Bank. China country-specific assistance strategy and plan (2004 – 2006), November 2003

[2] Asian Development Bank. China country-specific assistance strategy and plan (2004 – 2006), November 2003

[3] Jin Liqun. Introduction. In: Jin Liqun and Nicolas Stern, eds. Economic Development: Theories and Practice. Beijing: Economic sciences Press, 2002. p.25

[4] Steven Radelet. 2003, Challenging Foreign Aid. Center for Global Development, Washington, DC, Table 2.1

[5] World Bank. China country-specific assistance strategy (2003 – 2005). World Bank Group, January 2003; World Bank. China: Country assistance evaluation, operation evaluation department, December 29, R2003 – 0225, 2003; Asian Development Bank. China: Country assistance strategy and plan (2004 – 2006), November 2003

[6] Steven Radelet. Challenging Foreign Aid. Center for Global Development, Washington, DC, 2003. pp.132 – 137

5 Sectoral and Regional Analysis

5.1 Project Implementation Overview

IFI projects cover almost all the economic sectors in China and had made significant contributions to the economic development in every aspect of China.

First of all, the overall projects operations are very successful. Most of the projects have met the quantitative targets set during the project preparation and the implementations are very satisfactory, especially agriculture, energy and health projects. For eastern regions, IFI loans expanded financing channels for private enterprises through improved investment climate and operation environment, promoted the inflow of FDI and strengthened the integration with domestic and overseas markets. For central and western regions, IFI loans promoted inflow of capital through improving local infrastructure and changing development viewpoint and promoted the economic growth of the less developed regions.

Secondly, during the project implementation, project execution agencies emphasized on introducing foreign project management experiences, system innovation and building which, had positive external and demonstrative effects and provided rich experiences and lessons for projects of the same kind in project preparation, management, implementation and post evaluation. As a matter of fact, IFI project management, innovation in management system, and establishment of coordination mechanism for various levels of management agencies have all become the models for project operation of similar projects within the same sector.

Thirdly, viewed from the impact evaluation, IFI loans have very positive macro effects and played significant roles in social, economic, environmental, public service and public finance construction and development. Most of the IFI projects are for the public which have provided large volume of public goods, among which the implementation of basic infrastructure projects have greatly improved infrastructure, operation and investment climates of all regions, especially the central and western regions that lagged far behind in economic. They have significantly promoted the economic development of the less developed regions, increased the local per capita income and improved people's standard of living. Health and education projects reflected the developing viewpoint of people first and protected the interest of the disadvantaged group, improved the quality and working skills of the population, substantially increased public services and strengthened the capacities of the public institutes.

Finally, the success of the projects largely stems from improved international cooperation. Most of the IFI projects in China have technical assistance components and through various knowledge trainings, field trips and visits, achieved the dissemination of technology and externalities of traditions and systems. The evaluation result shows that the good performance of both the lenders and borrowers ensures a well implemented project. Through summarizing experiences of project constructions all over the world, IFIs set up a platform for sharing experiences. On the one hand, it had helped IFIs to improve their own project standard; on the other hand, experiences are shared among all the recipient countries thus significantly reduced the opportunity and social cost in project construction.

5.2 Lenders' Evaluation

The Quality Assurance Group (QAG) and the Operations Evaluation Department (OED) have made positive evaluation over most of the projects in China. According to QAG, the quality of supervision and project preparation in China have rose to the Bank average level, and in many cases above the average level. According to the evaluation of OED over the completed projects, China's percentage of satisfactory projects has remained way above the Bank average. The extraordinary performance can be credited to the high degree of state "ownership" of projects and the Chinese system of repayment obligations that require the direct beneficiaries repay the loans. Other project evaluations, including review of operations for poverty reduction, forestry, environment, involuntary resettlement related to river basin development, energy development and transportation, found strategies to be well directed generally and projects that either in whole or in part set the standard for best practice[1]. From the feedback of Chinese officials, representatives of implementation agencies and NGOs, it is found that although there are areas need improving, such as the high cost and complex procedures, the World Bank's assistance to China, especially the dissemination of knowledge and new viewpoint through loan and consulting activities have been highly appraised. This proved that IFI loans, such as the World Bank loans have brought with them the dissemination and spreading of knowledge and experiences in system and economic construction of other developing countries. These feedbacks conform to our evaluation.

According to ADB, China's portfolio is one of ADB's largest and best performing portfolios. China's portfolio performance is consistently better than the ADB average in terms of disbursement, contract awards, and most key project implementation indicators. This reflects China's strong state ownership, project implementation capability, and internal control systems. The evaluation showed that among the approved projects about 89% of the projects have met the project targets. These projects incorporated improved economic efficiency as one of the component for economic growth. Most of the projects have strengthened production capacity rather than improved productivity. Overall outcome of evaluation is based on the outcomes of particular objectives and on the relevance, efficacy, and efficiency of the Bank's assistance. The overall country assistance program evaluation rated the overall effect of ADB-supported projects as medium[2].

With China's economic development entering into different phases, IFI assistance strategies are changed and transformed accordingly with different focuses. Generally speaking, the projects emphasized capacity, institution and system building. For instance, among the 280 ADB supported technical assistance (TA) projects, consulting TA accounted for 73.2% of the total which were designed to provide technical assistance to various policy reforms. The key areas of the World Bank assistance strategy is mainly improving commercial environment, accelerating the transformation to a market-based economy, meeting the need of the poor, the disadvantaged and the regions that lagged behind and improving environmental protection to achieve sustainable development. Therefore, the key sectors for assistance have changed to transportation, city development (focused on reducing environmental pressure), social sector and energy sectors. The aim of ADB assistance strategy is to promote pro-poor economic growth. The priorities are to improve more fair and equal growth, normal market operation, improve environment and foster regional cooperation. Thus, the key sectors have changed to transportation, city infrastructure, agriculture and natural resources, energy and environment.

5.3 Sector Evaluation

Generally speaking, the implementation process of IFI projects in China is a inter-learning and inter-promoting process. It is very satisfactory in terms of social impacts, system building and environmental protection. The demonstration effects of these projects have provided valuable experiences for building similar projects in China in the future. However, it was also found that due to the insufficient understanding of project strategy and system arrangement of both the Chinese government and IFIs, the lender and borrower performance indicators are not satisfactory. From sectoral point of view, basically most of the IFI projects met their strategic objectives and the implementation is satisfactory and has positive impacts (Fig. 5.1). In the nine sectors that IFIs operates, seven are rated successful and above that accounted for 78% of total sectors among which agriculture, energy and health are the best and industrial and city construction are less satisfactory in terms of project performance.

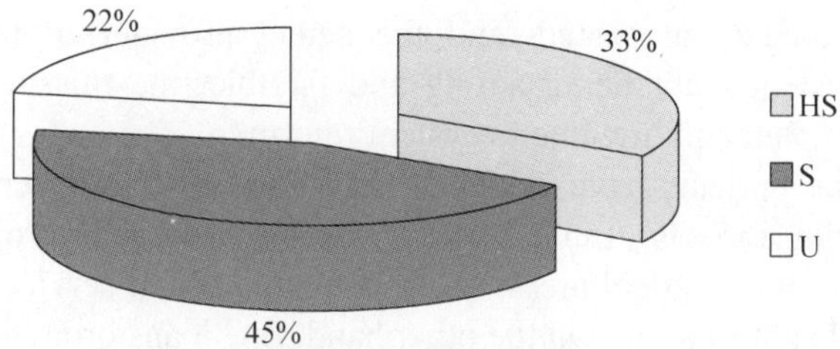

Figure 5.1 Level of project satisfaction by sector

Note: based on the performance of projects there are three levels of rating to represent the level of successfulness of the projects: HS (High Successful), S (Successful) and U (Unsuccessful)

Source: project report of the present project (micro section)

In terms of achieving project targets, transportation, health, water supply, and environmental protection, sectors are very good (Table 5.1). In these sectors, the design of the projects fits with the actual market conditions and actual needs of local residents. Meanwhile, the competitiveness of the projects themselves are very attractive to private investment and ensured the success of the projects.

Table 5.1 Project satisfactory level rating sheet by sector

	Target	Process	Outcome and impact
Agriculture	S	S	HS
Industry	HS	U	U
Energy	S	HS	HS
Transportation	HS	U	S
Education	U	HS	HS
Health	HS	S	S
Water Supply and Health	HS	U	S
City Construction	S	U	S
Environmental Protection	HS	U	HS
Overall Evaluation	HS	U	HS

Note: Targets are mainly to evaluate whether the specific targets set during the project preparation are met, especially quantitative targets; Process are mainly to evaluate management system, level of participation of the lender and borrower; Outcome and Impact are mainly to evaluate social benefits brought by the projects, including economic impact, environmental impact, social impact and project sustainability analysis, etc.

Source: Project report of the present project (Micro Section)

The energy and education sectors are very good in terms of project process control (Table 5.1). Both the sectors have very clear management institutions for projects that follow a strict management system, therefore easy to control. The project management entities maintained good cooperation with project implementation agencies. Various reasons have lead to unsatisfactory process control in most of the sectors. The main reasons include the mismatch of the designer of management system and the actual provider of the capital, the coordination system's not being strong and flexible, the missing of people in charge and in implementation due to system reform.

Most of the projects have achieved very good effects in terms of projects effects and social impacts (Table 5.1). On the one hand, the project targets are largely achieved, with agriculture, infrastructure and social service infrastructures being improved significantly. On the other hand, IFC loans brought with them the international management experiences, technology and new system arrangement, had very good demonstrative effects and provided large amount of experiences for similar projects in other regions. However, it is found that industrial projects are very competitive in themselves, and require high level of flexibility and ownership right, therefore, are not appropriate for using assistance loans. Although needed in national construction, industrial projects should be financed through other financing channels. This is one of the reasons that IFIs cut industrial projects sharply since the latter part of 1990s.

From the outcome of the evaluation, each of the sectors could be analyzed and the issues that need extra attention in future project implementation be pinpointed. In the authors' analysis, considering the similarities among city construction, city water supply and sanitation sectors, the two sectors are combined into one analysis.

5.3.1 Agriculture

The World Bank had provided US$9.7 billion loans to support a total of 61 agriculture development projects, while ADB supported 10 projects with US$547 million loans for rural and agriculture development. Most of these agriculture projects focus on agriculture supporting services, planting and agro-processing, forestry, irrigation and rural development. Meanwhile, agricultural projects usually targets to improve rural infrastructure and poverty reduction. The design of the agriculture projects is usually very complex with multiple targets.

The overall implementation of agriculture projects is relatively successful, the impact evaluation of the whole sector showed a very high level of success. Most of the projects have demonstrative effects and achieved the objective of reducing poverty and bridging the regional disparities. Some projects had made system innovation to achieve the project targets, such as establishing direct link between project implementation agencies with local research institutes, conducting timely mid-term project adjustment, therefore the projects are sustainable. These are the major reasons for the success of the projects.

However, due to the complexities of the projects and multi-targets of the projects, following issues are identified in the agriculture project implementation: (1) it is always difficult to implement commercial projects such as agro-processing projects; (2) some of the target design of the agriculture projects are so complex that they had to be changed significantly at mid-term adjustment when external conditions changed; (3) it is hard to protect ownership of privates' counterpart fund, thus the conflict during the project construction and repayment period had discouraged the implementation agencies; and (4) the coordination cost is pretty high when a project involves many entities. In addition, infrastructure, financial services, resources constraints and institution system had become constrains for the development of agriculture sector.

Therefore, for most of the regions, the focus of new agriculture projects will be on supporting agricultural sustainability, natural resources management, and rural development transition, rural financial system reform, institutional building and urbanization reform and transition, as well as protecting and directing the participation of private investors. But for western regions that are poor and lagged behind in development, the major tasks are to reduce poverty and improve infrastructure.

5.3.2 Industry

The World Bank has provided totaling US$2.845 billion loans to support 20 industrial projects, most of which were constructed during 1985 and 1995. The project focused on providing credits and industrial development. The major targets of the industrial projects are to bridge the gap in industry sectors and foreign exchange shortage and introduce foreign enterprise management experiences and the ideas of market-based economy. From this point of view, industrial projects are successful.

Industry sector is a competitive sector. Therefore, a lot of attention had been paid to the market demand during project design and it is relatively easy to attract private investors and easier to achieve project targets. However, a series of factors in physical operation had lead to the failure of the industrial projects: (1) the complex and time-consuming project approval procedure delayed market momentum and could not meet the changed market environment, projects lacked flexibility; (2) the project management system slowed the reaction of the project implementation entities to the market signal, the projects lacked adaptability and the management system is not efficient; and (3) projects acquired government credits from government agencies or state-owned enterprises and mismanagement is quite common.

Viewed from domestic investment, the percentage of state investment in the total investment is declining, especially the sharp reduction in the number of state-owned industrial projects, sets the trend for the change of IFI investment in industrial projects. In fact, industrial projects are typical competitive industry which requires clear definition of ownership and highly efficient monitoring and management models, however, the objectives of IFI loan projects are mainly focused on public interests. In order to achieve implementation efficiency, industrial projects should be operated in the commercial context. This is the reason that industrial projects declined sharply since the latter part of 1990s.

5.3.3 Energy

The energy sector developed very fast in China. In 2002, trailing the United States, China leaped to become the second largest generator of power. IFI energy projects are concentrated on thermo-power generation, for instance, among the 32 projects of US$6.434 billion loans supported by the World Bank, three quarters of the projects are focused on thermo-power generation. Renewable energy accounted for a very small proportion in power generation. Eighteen percent of ADB total loans were used to support 22 energy projects, which includes two private sector power projects. However, since the power supply and demand in the Chinese market stagnated, ADB reduced its assistance in this sector.

The overall implementation of energy projects is very successful. Energy sector is a mixed sector. On the one hand, it is competitive in project operation; on the other hand the projects benefit the public. Generally speaking, the performances of energy projects are successful in the following two aspects: (1) During the implementation of projects, both the lender and the borrower are actively participating in the projects, the management system were implemented effectively. It combined with the actual situation in China and accumulated experiences for state-owned enterprises and institutions, the experiences are disseminated extensively. Energy sector is one of the most effective sectors in light of the whole project implementation process. (2) Most of the energy projects achieved positive social impacts and to a certain degree assisted in creating new employment opportunities, increased local income and improved living standard.

However, when the energy projects were first designed they stressed heavily on thermo-power generation. It had adverse impact on environmental and ecological balance which in turn affected the production of power sector. Therefore, the focus of energy projects in the future is to change the objectives and means of production, control air-pollution, draft new policies to improve environment and supervisory system. The other focus would be to transmit energy to and improve energy infrastructure in the less developed regions.

5.3.4 Transportation

Since the three-port project in 1983, the World Bank had provided US$8.69 billion loans to construct 47 transportation projects that covered railways, roads and ports. The size of the portfolio in terms of total loans and number of projects is second to agriculture sector. The investment kept growing every year. These projects have provided support in training project execution inspectors, project control, design and planning, road safety, road surface management and major branches of national roads. From 1991, ADB had provided nearly US$4 billion loans to support 24 projects, among which ADB had provided direct funding for 3,200 kilometers of highway and bridge construction and helped improved 4,500 kilometers of local road network. Through providing direct investment and advisory technical assistance, ADB had played important role in mileage plan, road safety, human resources development, transportation pricing, commercialization and restructuring of transportation enterprises to attract private investment and supported the transportation infrastructure development.

Same as energy projects, transportation projects are mixed-type of projects. On the one hand, they improved local infrastructure, on the other hand they are highly competitive. Viewed from the project evaluation, transportation projects had promoted the infrastructure of project areas, improved local investment climate and bridged the gap in infrastructures of local governments, and therefore, received supports from local governments in system support and funds. Meanwhile, the characteristics of the projects themselves ensured self-circulation of fund of the projects. The implementation and operation of the transportation projects, on the one hand accumulated large volume of experiences in project management for the government, on the other hand, the projects brought in private investment improved investment climates of the regions where roads and railways passed, and played important roles in improving human resources quality.

However, the following issues in project design and operation need to be resolved: (1) insufficient feasibility study had been done for some projects during project preparation, and the complex approval procedures had missed market opportunity to certain degrees, thus some of the projects objectives are hard to achieve. During the preparation, noise pollution was not taken into consideration, therefore, the environmental benefits of the current transportation projects are very poor; (2) during project operation, due to the large size of capital involved, procurement and bidding procedures were implemented, financial transparency were ensured at the cost of efficiency, therefore, the coordination and supervision between the Chinese government and IFIs and among various government agencies need to be strengthened.

5.3.5 Education

The education project in 1981 is the first loan project of IFIs in China. Over the past two decades, the World Bank had awarded a total of US$1.697 billion loans to support 18 projects. Most of them were implemented during 1980s. Since 1990s, the loan declined every year, while the number of projects increased which focused on rural basic education, vocational training, and labor market development.

The overall implementation of education projects is highly successful, which mainly depended on good interaction between assisting agencies and implementation agencies and the dissemination and spread of knowledge and technology brought about by large amount of trainings and technical assistance. However, due to the significant difference among regions and different level of education, as well as impacts of the gradually accelerated education system reform on the projects, it is difficult to set a standard targets for education sector projects, thus not likely to be repeatable.

Owing to the fast development in education, the demand for education has changed. Thus projects should be designed according to the needs of different regions and adopt different assistance measures. This requires that both the lenders and borrowers design the project targets and assistance strategies based on the actual situations of different regions while maintaining a good project management system and strengthening cooperation with other institutions and departments to disseminate project achievements and experiences. The focus of education project should be changed to universal rural education and re-employment training for urban population, as well as the development of the third education.

5.3.6 Health

The first health project of the World Bank in China was the rural health and medical education project in 1984. Over the past two decades, the World Bank had provided a total of US$940 million loans to support 11 projects focusing on communicable disease control in less developed rural areas, infant and maternal health care and basic health services.

The overall implementation of health projects is very good which conformed to the key areas of local governments and provided the capital and technology, as well as experiences and knowledge of other countries that were badly needed in local development of such public sectors. The actively participation of local government had increased the population that benefited from the project and played a very important role in improving the quality of population. Most of the health projects are highly sustainable and self-financing, and the medical system and practice that constructed in early projects are still operating in the basic health sectors.

Health projects also face the same problem as most of the public goods sectors of low economic efficiency, therefore under great pressure for debt repayment. Another issue need to be resolved is how to introduce private investment into health sector. With the social progress, the focuses of health sector projects in the future should be communicable disease control, public medical and health system building, and establishing and improving urban and rural health insurance system, etc.

5.3.7 City Construction, Water Supply and Environmental Sanitation

Most of the city construction, including water supply and environmental sanitation projects were constructed during 1990s. There has been an increasing trend of projects and capital which is highly related to the accelerated urbanization in China. Since 1985, the World Bank had provided US$2.288 billion loans to support 24 projects of city construction, water supply and environmental sanitation in China. Although the projects were not very large, all of them were designed to solve the city environment problems, emphasized on waste water treatment and saving energy and had achieved the expected results. Since 1988, ADB had provided US$34 million loans for 50 technical assistance projects. These development construction and technical assistance projects were focused on researches on water resource management, environmental protection, water supply and waste water treatment and assisted the government to strengthen the drafting of water resources management policy and strategy.

The objectives of the city construction projects are to solve the bottleneck problems that might lead to the rising of production and transaction costs, improve the development of city industrial and services sectors; to address the city environmental issues and reduce poverty; to improve the urban residents' living conditions and standard to minimize the negative effects of city expansion without proper planning. The city waste water treatment and health projects were mainly designed to address the problems of the low level of per capita water usage, flood, long-term draughts, and seasonal changes, the large disparity among cities and provinces in the disposable water resources, and try to meet the increasing demand for clean water supply and related city services stem from the fast-pace economic development.

Overall, the project implementation of these two sectors is not very successful. To a certain degree, this was resulted from lack of implementation experiences with fewer projects and short period of time. However, it also reflected some issues: (1) During project preparation, there has been insufficient understanding of actual issues that different cities and different regions are facing. Thus too much competitive sub-project components were designed in the projects. (2) The coordination among government agencies needs to be further improved. Most of the projects in the two sectors are comprehensive projects producing public goods which involved many government agencies and had multiple targets. Therefore, coordination capability among participating agencies became the key constraint for the performance of the projects. Also, most of the project targets are long-term objectives that targeted to protect the disadvantaged group and promote equality, thus conflict with short-term goals of develop resources and speed up urbanization, and affect some interest groups. Therefore, it is very important as to how to better coordinate the interests of different interest groups in the project implementation.

5.3.8 Environmental Protection

With the economic development in China, sustainable development has become the development theme. IFIs like the World Bank and ADB have all made environmental protection and achieving sustainable development their major assistance strategy. Since the Tianjin City Development and Environmental Protection Project in 1992, within only 12 years, the World Bank has provided a total of US$2.352 billion loans and supported 19 projects to improve environment in China. Meanwhile, agriculture, energy, transportation, and city construction projects all added environmental requirements and provided environmental technical assistance. ADB had provided US$2.7 billion loans to improve environment, among which US$2.1 billion loans were used to address "black" pollution problem, US$600 million loans to address "green" problems. Loans related to environment accounted for nearly one quarter of ADB total loans to China. ADB also provided 119 technical assistance projects related to environment with a total of over US$77 million loans. These projects and funds were mainly focused on enhancing environmental policies and supervision, developing market mechanism, strengthening capacity building of related agencies, and promoting natural resources protection and disseminating clean technologies, etc. They have provided external help in environmental management and investment and had established partnership in many areas. For instance, renewable energy research and development, clean production dissemination, city and rural medical and health infrastructure construction, land degradation prevention, encouraging local groups participation in environmental management, and environmental policies and system reform.

The evaluation showed that the targets of the environmental protection projects conformed to the development strategies of the project areas and largely achieved the multiple targets of protecting environment, maintaining eco-balance, conserving water and soil, and improving the soil quality. In the meanwhile, they have played important roles in the decision-making of environment related policies and system reform, enterprise production and strategic choices. The technical assistance in the future should be focused on how to make the rules and policies set by the project implementation agencies more acceptable to the market, how to establish a penalty and restrictive mechanism that penalizes and restricts wrong behaviors during the implementation of the projects. The clean resources and natural resources projects experiences show that the projects need careful financial feasibility study and benefits sustainability study. For those projects with lower financial rate of returns but high economic and environmental benefits to the public, we should explore to establish a fiscal mechanism to provide necessary assistance through transferring payment.

For most of the sectors, the overall performance has high level of success in terms of achieving project targets, management system, social impacts and sustainability (Table 5.2). This reflects that most of the IFI loan projects are

Table 5.2 Sub-indicator sheets of the project evaluation

Evaluation indicators	Good	Bad	Issues and experiences
Targets	Industry, transportation, health and environmental protection		1. the project targets did not conform with actual situation and national development strategy, since they have to give way to other projects and priorities in the implementation process; 2. external market change and policy changes make it difficult to achieve project targets.
Management system	Agriculture, water supply and sanitation, city construction	Energy, transportation, and education	1. most of the projects introduced new system arrangement and system design that had demonstrative effects, in which the experiences accumulated will benefit other projects; 2. efficiency and capital losses due to changes in implementation agencies and responsible agencies.
Lenders performance	Energy, education and health	Industry, transportation and city construction	1. the lower level of participation of IFIs in project selection and feasibility study, lead to series of problems; 2. mid-term adjustment had played very important roles; 3. the experts provided supports to the project process, financial and technical aspects, but also lead to rigidity and lagged-reaction.
Borrowers performance	Transportation and education	Agriculture, water supply, environmental protection, and city construction	1. counterpart funds played important roles, but generally the percentage of counterpart is low and not in place; 2. the borrowers had made efforts to promote projects, and to work with local research institutes is a new system innovation; 3. repayment system has not been established.

Continued

Evaluation indicators	Good	Bad	Issues and experiences
Economic benefits	Large scale transportation, energy infrastructure projects	Public goods sectors such as Health, education, environmental protection, complete competitive sector such as industry, and mixed sector of agriculture	1. weak in project implementation and counterpart funding; 2. most of the regions, lack the ability to mobilize the economic resources.
Environmental benefits	Environmental protection and agriculture	Transportation	1. project strategy emphasized on environmental protection policies; 2. the environmental protection is directly related to the local economic development models.
Social benefits	Agriculture, health and transportation		1. IFI projects, especially projects that produce public goods ensured the extensiveness of the benefiting groups, however, there is a gap between urban and rural areas and among regions; 2. the projects had significant social pulling effects, however, the impact on improving public services is very limited and also very weak in promoting private investment and participation; 3. projects emphasized on physical construction, neglecting research.
Sustainability	Agriculture, health, and education	Industry	1. most of the projects established supervision system to maintain the project implementation, however when the project completed or ended the disbursement, most of the mechanism are not functional any more, and the project are in the state of stagnation; 2. most of the projects do not have appropriate risk averse mechanism, not capacity to withstand the policy changes and external environmental changes.

Source: Project Reports (micro report section).

successful and largely conformed to China's sectoral development strategic targets. When the loan closed at the end of the projects, most of the targets had been achieved. These projects had very good demonstrative effects on our economic construction. They changed people's viewpoint and behaviors in some way, changed government expenditure models and enhanced transfer payment, which in turns strengthened the adjustment role of government, and accumulated lessons and valuable experiences for system arrangement in future project implementation.

The successful projects are the projects where the performance of both lenders and borrowers are good. This implicated that the communication and coordination capacities of both the lenders and borrowers need to be further improved. Multilateral cooperation is very necessary. This is a challenge for Chinese government and corresponding project implementation agencies, and it is also a driving force for institutional reform and efficiency improvement.

5.4 Regional Evaluation

The geographic distribution of IFI projects are changed in the same pace with government policies and strategic adjustment. During 1980s and the first half of 1990s, the World Bank and ADB loan assistance concentrated along the coastal regions which was determined by the government's strategy of developing coastal areas. Later, the assistance recipient regions changed as the government adjusted its development policy and strategy, a result of mutual coordination (Table 5.3).

Table 5.3 The World Bank loans regional distribution in China

Region	1980 – 1990		1990 –	
	Loan (US$10,000)	Percentage (%)	Loan (US$10,000)	Percentage (%)
East	3,739.76	53.89	9,670.56	42.38
West	1,961.54	28.27	8,208.52	35.98
Central	1,238.15	17.84	4,937.53	21.64
Total	6,939.45	100	22,816.61	100

Source: the World Bank Mission in China, The World Bank Projects in China by Sectors, http://www.worldbank.org.cn/Chinese/Projects/projects_all_dept.asp.

Generally speaking, the project implementation in eastern and western regions is better than that in the central regions (Table 5.4). The number of projects collected in the samples for the present study is not equally distributed among regions which might result in some level of bias in evaluation. However, some internal objective reasons can be found for this regional disparity in project performance.

Table 5.4 Level of success of the projects by region

Region	Target	Economic	Environ-mental	System	IFI participation	Borrowers participation	Overall evaluation
East	High	High	Medium	High	High	High	High
West	Medium	Low	Low	Low	Low	Low	Low
Central	Low	Medium	High	Medium	Medium	Medium	Medium

Source: Project Reports (Micro Reports Section).

Over the past two decades, IFI projects gradually moved away from the increasingly rich coastal regions to the less developed western regions. The eastern regions had accumulated large amount of experiences in project construction and management, and had formulated more efficient management system and rules and regulations that could provide very good guidance for the newly approved projects. Meanwhile, the eastern regions had passed the development phase of resource predatory development. Common consensus has been reached in environmental protection and sustainable development and had become the main theme and of economic development.

It was until several recent years that the western regions started to receive IFI loans. Western regions learned from the lessons and experiences of the eastern regions in project design, construction and management. In this period, IFI had adjusted their assistance strategy to China, and most of the projects in the western regions are in infrastructure and public service sectors, which conformed to the local regional development strategy, therefore, the overall operation is very successful.

As far as the central regions are concerned, this region is still at the starting stage of industrialization, and the local development targets favored more of the industrial and transportation projects that might bring more economic benefits. The government and private investors are not enthusiastic in participating in agriculture, education and health projects. To a certain degree, this conflicts with the IFI assisting strategy. In addition, institutional restructuring in this region had resulted in dramatic changes in the institutions, which is a negative factor in the project operation.

References

[1] The World Bank. China country assistance strategy. 2003

[2] ADB. China country strategy and program. 1998

6 The Roles and Contributions of IFI Loans to China

The study evaluated the IFI loans to China against the broader background of China's economic reform. In summary, the IFI loans played three important roles and made six significant contributions to the development in China.

6.1 Three Important Roles

6.1.1 Seed Money Role

The loan assistance of the World Bank and ADB to China during 1980s provided "seed money" badly needed in China's economic construction in time and brought with them the international experience and knowledge that promoted the market-based economic reform in China. China was at early stage of economic take-off with insufficient construction capital and development knowledge. The international financial assistance loans were mainly used to help China break the development and knowledge bottlenecks. As former Vice Minister of Finance, Jin Liqun pointed out "the IFI assistance is not only a very important source of foreign capital that provided significant support to China's economic construction, their rich knowledge and practical experience in economic development brought new knowledge and new concepts to the Chinese economic reform [1]."

Since 1990s, domestic private investment and foreign direct investment increased dramatically, thus the capital shortage in China has been eased significantly. Although the percentage of international financial assistance loans in total domestic investment decreased, the "knowledge" relationship between China and IFIs became increasingly important [2]. These institutions provided China with development knowledge and technical assistance and played a role of "Knowledge Bank" and reform-monger in assisting Chinese Government promoting economic reform.

6.1.2 Demonstrative Role

Different from private investment projects or any other prior government invested projects, the World Bank and ADB projects are based on comprehensive development framework (CDF), country assistance strategy (CAS), and country strategy and program (CSP) that emphasize the demonstrative effects and externalities of the projects. Successful assistance projects can bring in new technology, new management skills, new system innovation and good policy recommendations and the effects can be multiplied through demonstration and learning. Since these projects were carefully designed to conform to the development strategy of the Chinese Government, they have strong demonstrative effects that were repeatable and reproducible. In general, they played an effective role in the project preparation and implementation process across sectors, regions and industries, as well as cross-cutting areas. In addition, IFIs continued to accumulate good experience in project implementation, identify and solve problems, develop advanced development viewpoints, project management, project coordination mechanism, special development capability and internal and external knowledge of the projects. The projects had very high success and client satisfaction rate and are implemented timely, which provided valuable demonstrative models for development in different regions and sectors.

The villages participated in the World Bank Southwest Poverty Project benefited from the projects dramatically in poverty reduction comparing with villages that participated in government sponsored projects. Such projects not only had demonstrative effects, but also had competition effects. The public will naturally ask why there is difference between World Bank project villages and comparing villages and what can we learn from it? (Table 6.1)

Table 6.1 Comparing some of the indicators between World Bank southwest poverty project villages and comparing villages (1995 – 2000)

	Project villages		Comparing villages	
	1995	2000	1995	2000
1. Poverty degree				
Incidence rate	31.5	17.7	21.0	13.0
Depth indicator	5.8	3.6	3.3	2.5
Severity indicator	1.23	1.11	0.50	0.73
2. Food safety				
Per capita food consumption (kilogram)	189.2	209.4	199.6	216.5
Percentage with food safety	82.3	95.6	82.8	95.1
3. Villages with accessibility to material property (%)				
Electricity	75.2	98.2	94.3	100.0
Road	82.3	96.4	87.4	97.7
Water		65.1		71.4

Continued

	Project villages		Comparing villages	
	1995	2000	1995	2000
4. Accessibility to social services (%)				
Percentage of villages with elementary school	92.0	94.7	93.1	96.6
Enrollment rate for pupils between 7 – 12	89.0	90.6	93.6	97.0
Gender gap indicator for pupil enrolled between 7 – 12	91.1	96.6	96.7	98.2
Percentage of pupil under 15 completed elementary education	49.5	70.5	60.2	79.4
Percentage of villages with clinic	26.5	84.1	20.7	69.0
Percentage of villages with village doctors	45.1	89.4	50.6	79.3
Percentage of villages with qualified midwife	25.7	80.5	39.1	78.2
Percentage of women gave birth at hospital/clinic	4.1	14.9	9.8	19.1
5. Self-development Capability				
Percentage of labors work in other places	7.9	12.0	6.6	11.7
Per capita cash and saving (Yuan)	93.2	351.8	135.2	496.0

Source: January 1, 2004, Wu Guobao, A Case Study on China Southwest Poverty Project.

6.1.3 Catalyst Role

IFIs adjusted their assistance strategies with the change of Chinese Government's strategy from time to time in order to conform to China's development plan and support the implementation of Chinese Government's development strategy. A healthy coordination mechanism has been developed in broader international cooperation, including bilateral and multilateral dialogue mechanism. The coordination and interaction between IFIs and the Chinese government provided strong support for China to achieve a win-win for China and the world, and had played a role of "catalyst".

The loan assistance has in part directly promoted the development of recipient regions and improved the living standard of the recipient people in many ways, such as providing necessary basic infrastructure, improving basic living condition, and creating better investment climate. The technical assistance and advisory technical assistance (ADTA) have disseminated knowledge. As a matter of fact, the IFI assistance loans not only considered the economic benefits and investment returns, but also emphasized on making good use of the projects to promote development and reform in related sectors. The policy recommendations of the World Bank to the Chinese Government are reflected in its reports, such as

Country Assistance Strategy, Comprehensive Development Framework, and Poverty Reduction Strategy Report. These policy recommendations provided guidance for China in developing macro economic policies and development policies to improve resources utilization and reduce poverty.

The above three roles reflected a healthy relationship of mutual cooperation and promotion between Chinese Government and IFIs and the achievement of a development goal of mutually beneficiary and win-win for all parties. The collaboration between Chinese government and the IFIs had followed a right direction with right method and is on right track. The experience has been summarized timely and disseminated broadly (Box 6.1).

Box 6.1 The World Bank assistance and China's reform

After experimented with various planned-economy reforms for 30 years, China was still a low income country when it started market-based reform by the end of 1970s. Independent research shows that interaction between the World Bank and China had significant impact on maintaining reform dynamic. During 1980s, the World Bank for the first time provided in-depth and comprehensive analysis on Chinese economic development and studies on some key department reforms to the senior policy makers. The World Bank also assisted the reformers strengthen their confidence and determinations, recommended some specific policies and systems, they also provided training for government officials to learn market-based economy skills (from project financing to international procurement). The World Bank provided technical assistance to assist China to fit in the outside world; such assistance includes aspects from recommendations on liberalizing trade and merging exchange rate, to assisting port modernization. In short, the World Bank served as a trustworthy advisor to the Chinese Government when China held skeptical attitude toward the outside world. This had laid a foundation for private investment which later became the backbone for China's success.

The reform in China became the largest poverty reduction operation, especially wiping out the extreme poverty in rural areas. Benefited from 65 rural development projects supported by the World Bank and joint efforts of many departments, rural poverty reduced dramatically (number of poor in total population reduced from 34% in 1985 to 18% in 1998), including researches designed to identify and confirm the actual reasons for the change in rural poverty. The World Bank collaborated with social departments in China, especially a series of large scale basic education and health projects, have made significant contribution to the sustained development in human resources and development indicators. The World Bank's policy recommendations and financial support assisted China developed infrastructure that is closely related to economic growth and formulated sector policies which include the transportation policy that promotes market integration and the energy policies in particular. Finally, one of the major progresses made in the Bank's assistance to China in the past decade was that it helped China formed and established a more solid national environment agenda.

Through the whole process of the World Bank's operation in China (China has been the largest client of the World Bank in policy advisory services and investment support), the Chinese government have showed a very high level of responsibility. The key indicator is that the project implementation agencies have consistently been among the best performance agencies in the World Bank.

Source: Ian Goldin, Halsey Rogers, and Nicholas Stern. *The Role and Effectiveness of Development Assistance: Lessons from World Bank Experience*. Washington: World Bank

6.2 Six Significant Contributions

6.2.1 Development Viewpoint Contribution

The most significant contribution that IFIs loan made to China is its development viewpoint. The success of development strategy is the biggest success and the most effective success. China is a big developing country with the largest population. The number one task for the Chinese government has been to accelerate development. However, at the beginning of the reform, China did not know much about many important issues related to development, such as what should be the development aims, what development targets need to be achieved, what development strategies should be adopted, and what is China's development viewpoint. IFIs presented their development theories and policy researches to the Chinese government for reference and had made positive influence on the change of the development viewpoint and development strategy (Fig. 2). Since 1960s, the world development viewpoint experienced a change from "pro-growth" or "growth-based" development to "targeted social development", to "sustainable development" (1992, the World Bank and United Nation), to "comprehensive Development" (1999, the World Bank), to "Millennium Development Goals" (2002, United Nation). This is the important international background for Chinese government to develop a development viewpoint of people first and promoting reform and innovation in accordance with the "five balanced aspects" (the Third Session of the Sixteenth National Congress of the Communist Party of China, 2003).

The World Bank Country Assistance Strategy has also changed from promoting economic growth and transition, promoting financial and private sector development, and management reform of physical institutions to a new century strategy that focuses on improving investment and operation climate, accelerating transition to market-based economy, meeting the needs of poor and disadvantaged people and the development of regions that lagged behind, and promoting sustainable development. The assistance strategy of the ADB also experienced two phases and each emphasized different focuses. The first phase is from 1986 to 1990 during which the Chinese government was responsible for directing the submission of projects to ADB, thus there was limited room for ADB to develop appropriate country strategy and play a more leading role. The second phase started in 1991 during which the ADB operation in China expanded quickly. In 1991, ADB developed the very first country operation strategy targeting China. During this period, there are mainly three strategic targets, namely "improving economic efficiency, reducing poverty and protecting environment and natural resources[3]."

Recently, the World Bank and ADB developed new assistance strategy and program respectively and identified their major development sectors to conform to priority sectors of the Chinese government (Table 8.2).

6.2.2 Pulling Investment Contribution

The contribution to pulling investment can be described as two major contributions. One is the contribution to direct investment which is the direct effect of IFI investment. During 1980's, the Chinese government actively utilized foreign loans that include IFI loans to meet the shortage in capital for domestic construction. The assistance loans accounted for 26% – 28% of the total foreign capital during 1980's. During the Seventh Five-Year Plan period, assistance loan was 23.1% of the total domestic budgetary investment. The percentage of assistance loans in total domestic budgetary investment remained pretty high even during 1990's. For instance, the percentage was as high as 60.3% and 30.1% during the eighth and ninth five-year plan period and respectively. This reflects that the ratio of budgetary capital in total fixed asset investment has been declining since 1980's from 28.1% in 1981, to 8.7% in 1990 and 6.4% in 2000. To a large extent, IFIs loans bridged the gap in public investment.

The other contribution is indirect investment, which means that the IFI investment induced more investment. The present study found that IFI loans had positive impacts in inducing FDI and private investment. The underlying reason for this effect is that the IFI loans have been used to provide public products and services which improved the investment environment in China, hence attracting private capital. The inducing effects of IFI funds is a self-intensifying process, which played a catalyst role in attracting private funds so as to realize sustainable economic growth (see Box 6.2).

Box 6.2 The investment pulling effects of IFI loans

1. Promoting the Chinese economic growth in 90s: In 80s, every one percentage point of increase in IFI loans contributed to economic growth by – 14.1%. After 1990, IFI loans increased by one percentage point, the economic growth rate increased by 5.5%.

2. Promoting the economic growth in less developed areas: The positive impacts of IFI loans on the economic development in the western areas are substantial. IFI loan increased by one percentage point in the western areas, the economic growth rate increased 4.45%, while IFI loans increased by one percentage point in the central areas, the growth rate increased around 1.3%.

3. Facilitating the long term growth of the economy: IFI loans increased by one percentage point, in the next five years, the average accumulative contribution to the economic growth will be 8.39%.

4. Promoting the long term growth of private investment: IFI loans increased by one percentage point, private investment will increase by 14.88% accumulatively and social total investment by 2.2% in the next five years.

5. Promoting the increase of saving rate in the eastern areas: IFI loans increased by one percentage point, the saving rates in the eastern areas were increased 3.05%, while it had no or even negative impacts to the saving rates in the central and western areas.

6. Promoting the FDI inflow to the eastern areas: Every Yuan of increase of IFI loans to eastern areas attracted FDI 4.8 Yuan in the same year, 1.8 Yuan in the next year while IFI loans had minimum impacts on FDI inflow into central and western areas.

Source: 2004, Hu Angang and Wang Qingrong, Catalyst for Promoting Growth and Attracting Investment: Macro Economic Evaluation over IFI Loans to China (1981 – 2001), Center For China Study Working Paper.

During economic transition, public finance will gradually exit from competitive, profit-making, and non public investment sectors and focus on the public and infrastructure sectors, in which IFI loans have played an important promoting role. First, since the decentralization, the fiscal capacity (the weight of fiscal revenue to GDP), especially that of the central government, has dropped dramatically, and the inflow of the IFI funds timely bridged the gap in public investment to some extend which helped the transition of fiscal system. Second, from the end of 1980's, the lasting and high-level budget deficits have always been constraining the long-term public investment. In fact, from late 1980's to mid 1990's, the fiscal investment kept falling which did not turn around until 1996. IFI loans, as one of the international deficit financing measures, have the advantages of long repayment terms which ease the short and mid-term pressure for domestic deficit financing.

6.2.3 Infrastructure Construction Contribution

IFI loans have played important roles in transportation, urban development, energy, water supply and waste water treatment sectors. At the beginning of 1980's, the infrastructure in China lagged behind the economic development. China had experienced shortage in water, power and energy supply. As pointed out in the Report of the Twelfth National Congress of the Communist Party of China, there had been a severe distress in energy and transportation. The transportation capacity could not meet the need of the increased transportation volume (1992, Hu Yaobang). At that time, China did not even have one highway. By the end of 2002, the total mileage of road in China was 1.8 million kilometers (km), which includes 25,100 km highway. China, next to US, became the country with the second longest highway system. In 1980, the total coal production was 630 million tons which increased by 63% in 1990 and doubled in 2002. Power generation doubled, among which hydro power increased by 1.2 times. The city water supply capacity increased by 22.6% over the ten years during 1990's. Infrastructure improved substantially, and city infrastructure such as road and water supply increased by different degrees (Table 6.2).

Table 6.2 Infrastructure construction development in China (1980 – 2002)

	1980	1985	1990	1995	2000	2002
Railroad (10,000 km)	5.33	5.50	5.78	5.97	6.87	7.19
Road (10,000 km)	88.33	94.24	102.83	115.70	140.27	176.52
Highway (10,000 km)			0.05	0.21	1.63	2.51
Civil aviation	19.53	27.72	50.68	112.90	150.29	163.77
Annum total water supply (100 million tons)	88.3	128.0	382.3	496.6	469.0	466.5
Total energy production (10,000 ton standard coal)	63,735	85,546	103,922	129,034	106,988	139,000

Since 1985, the World Bank have provided a total of US$5.3 billion loans for 22 road and six city transportation projects. These projects have supported human resources development in project execution inspection, quality control, design and plan, road safety, road management and main section of national road. Since 1991, ADB has provided nearly US$4 billion for 2,473 projects that built 3,200 km highway and bridges. These projects also improved local road network of 4,500 km and has built a total 70,100 km of railroad.

In railway transportation sector, the World Bank mainly participated in expanding the national railway network capacity. Since 1984, the World Bank has provided a total of US$2.2 billion loans for 8 national railway projects and 1 local railroad project. Since 1989, ADB has provided nearly US$1.6 billion loans to 10 projects that assisted the construction of 8 local railways with total mileage of 2,301 km and three national railway projects with increment of 3,484 km in railway mileage. All these projects have adopted advanced technologies and improved the operational efficiency through system reform and restructuring.

6.2.4 Poverty Reduction Contribution

IFIs have always attached great importance to the inequality problems in China and made great efforts in eliminating the development inequality among regions and between urban and rural areas. Both the World Bank and ADB have assisted China in developing various anti-poverty strategies during different periods of time, and helped China summarize experience and disseminate Chinese poverty reduction experiences. The World Bank and ADB had made contributions and efforts in (1) appealing Chinese government's attention to the poor and the disparity between the rich and the poor; (2) project financing aimed at poor people; and (3) introducing effective poverty reduction mechanism.

One of the greatest achievements of Chinese government in reform was that poverty population was massively reduced. Using the World Bank measurement of poverty, US$1 per day income and expenditure, the total poverty population was reduced from 490 million in 1990 to 204 million in 2000. Percentage of poverty in total population was reduced from 51% in 1980 to 16% in 2000 (Table 1.1).

6.2.4.1 Advocating for Paying Attention to the Poor and the Increasing Disparity between the Rich and the Poor

Since 1984, the World Bank had published many research papers identifing the problems in China's development and corresponding schemes to solve these problems. They directed their attention to the problems of the disparity between the rich and the poor and the problem of the poor become poorer. They are the important advocates for pushing the Chinese government to enhance its poverty reduction efforts[①]. The World Bank and ADB promoted the change of Chinese government poverty reduction policies through the followings:

Introducing new development viewpoint. The publications of the World Bank and ADB are extensively related to the ideas of people first, equal development and pro-poor growth, and helped the Chinese academia to become the advocates of the poor by providing a new research framework and source of ideas. Concepts, such as "disadvantaged group", "poor and rich disparity" (such as GINI coefficient), were formally introduced into the Government work reports and caught the attention of the news and media.

① The World Bank's assistance helped the Chinese Government to the poverty reduction through the following 5 approaches: promote employment and production efficiency; accelerate the domestic market integration; invest in people, improve human development indicators and social development indicators; link various projects with poverty reduction.

Providing technical assistance and making knowledge contribution to build social safety net. It is a major indicator for a modern civilized country to set up wide coverage social security net, and also the most effective mechanism to protect the rights of the poor. IFIs (especially the World Bank) helped in financing the related studies and implementing the pilot projects to gain experiences.

6.2.4.2 Implemented Pro-Poor Poverty Reduction Projects

The most direct contribution that the World Bank and ADB made to the poor is that they have implemented large number of projects targeted for poverty reduction which involved many sectors and regions. These poverty reduction projects have helped the poor to achieve human development in the following three areas:

Firstly, providing the poor access to sustainable means of production locally, including capital, land, fuel, and market. This is the most effective short-term and medium-term poverty reduction measures. There are many means to achieve this, for instance, improve agricultural infrastructure that includes upgrading soil, building irrigation ditches, constructing rural roads, etc. to increase the output directly (Box 6.3); provide micro-credit to the farmers in combination with market information services to bring the farmers closer to the market and change their ways of production and increase income. One of the World Bank's focuses was to reduce the poverty of the recipient regions and people. The World Bank had supported 61 agriculture projects with US$9.7 billion loans. While ADB tried to reduce poverty directly or indirectly through supporting agriculture sector. ADB has supported 10 agriculture and rural development projects in China with a total of US$547 million loans.

Box 6.3 Infrastructure and poverty reduction

Adequate infrastructure is a prerequisite for reducing poverty. Estimates show that (1) every RMB 10,000 invested in building roads will lift 3.2 persons on average out of poverty; (2) per capital road length increased by 1%, household consumption will increase by 0.08%; (3) irrigation spending increase by 1%, agriculture output per farmer will increase by 0.41%, and poverty rate will reduce by 1.13% and (4) every RMB 10,000 invested in power construction will lift 2.3 persons on average out of poverty.

The following mechanisms make the infrastructure effective in poverty reduction: improved road will promote the agriculture and non-agriculture development, including provided more opportunities for rural population (including the poor); targeted interventions to local conditions and involving the participation of local communities increase the likelihood of success of road projects; the construction of first class road and village road, as well as investment in agricultural research, education, power and communication will promote economic growth and reduce poverty; although the cost for constructing second class road per kilometer is much lower than that for first class road, the marginal effects of investing in constructing second class road is much bigger.

Source: November 2003, Asian Development Bank: *China Country Strategy and Program* (2004 – 2006).

Secondly, created more employment opportunities for the poor. According to econometrics analysis, the IFI loans to central and western regions can effectively increase private investment and growth. The benefits of economic growth to the poor are not limited to the provision of markets for agricultural products, most importantly, growth provides more employment opportunities for the poor and increases their income directly. During the implementation of IFI loan projects, infrastructure construction would need large number of labors, while the private investment attracted by the improved infrastructure will provide employment for the rural population with some education in processing and service sectors; the improved transportation will increase the mobility of the poor, expand their employment geographically and increased their source of information, increase the likelihood for employment and reduced cost.

Thirdly, directly or indirectly made human resources development that gave core dynamic to the poor regions to get rid of poverty distress. To the people living in poor regions, besides farming and limited simple labor intensive employment opportunities, human resource development is the single most effective way to increase social mobility and sharing of the benefits of social economic development. There are also many ways to improve human capital, among which education is the investment with the most far reaching benefits. Over the past two decades, the World Bank had implemented over 10 cross-provincial rural education projects, including normal education project, curriculum project, basic education in poor regions project, labor development project, and vocational education, etc. Many of the poor drop-out children returned to school due to the system change, and the teacher quality and teaching condition improved in rural areas. All the implementation of the projects included large amount of training in which accumulatively over millions of people have been trained. These trainings improved the knowledge level of the poor. In addition, the environmental protection projects, public health projects and clean drinking water projects in rural areas protected the living condition of the poor and improved their health.

6.2.4.3 Introduced Effective Poverty Reduction System

The World Bank is a multilateral international development institute that has accumulated extensive experiences all over the world over the past 40 years. ADB is very familiar with the economic, geographic and cultural environment in Asia and is also very experienced. Both the World Bank and ADB have introduced to China many effective poverty reduction experiences proved in other countries. The poverty reduction measures therefore have changed from poverty relief of the mid 1980s to poverty reduction through development. Since 1994, a system of poverty alleviation to town, to village and to household have been implemented.

IFIs have played an active role in this process, such as introducing double-dimensional poverty reduction strategy and the idea of reducing poverty through participation, as well as effective poverty reduction measures of providing micro-credit to the poor. IFIs also assisted China developed localized poverty reduction measures based on actual situation and experiences, such as the widely implemented infant and mother safety project, rural household capacity building projects, etc. A healthy two-way cooperation between IFIs and China's poverty reduction cause has been developed that strengthened China's poverty reduction capability, among which China Southwest Poverty Reduction Project is the most successful model for cooperation (Box 6.4).

Box 6.4 A case study of China southwest poverty reduction project

The Project Targets are Achievable

From macro point of view, the Southwest Poverty Reduction project not only achieved national poverty reduction goal, but also reflected international equal development goal and the target of building a moderately prosperous society. In March 1994, the Chinese government developed National Eighth Five-Year Plan Poverty Reduction Plan, in which it was clearly pointed out a poverty reduction goal of "providing over 80 million people without enough food and wear with enough food and clothing in seven years from 1994 to 2000". The Chinese Government and the World Bank started to prepare for the China Southwest Poverty Reduction Project in 1993 which was designed to experiment with the new theory and idea of using large amount of IFI loans to reduce poverty in a large geographical area through international cooperation.

From micro point of view, the Southwest Poverty Reduction Project is designed to solve the poverty distress of the poor farmers in project areas. The southwest poverty region is one of the key areas for national poverty reduction, the poor people living in this region accounts for 53% of the total poverty population. This project covers 36 counties, 281 towns and 2,424 villages that directly benefit about 2.5 million people. The six major targets set in the projects are basically achieved. Among which the targets of per capita income, elementary school enrollment and completion rate, infant mortality rate, local epidemic incidence rate and number of towns and villages with access to road are achieved beyond the level preset during project preparation, the target of per capita basic farmland was also basically achieved.

Why Can the Project Reduce Poverty in Large Scale

The coordination and collaboration of the economy, the society, the market and the government at both macro and micro levels contributed to the significant effects of the Southwest Poverty Reduction Project. During the project implementation, the poverty incidence rate, poverty depth, and poverty re-occurrence rate were reduced by 13.8, 2.2, and 10 percentage points respectively. At macro level, the effective combination of national poverty reduction strategy and advanced international poverty reduction experiences had laid scientific and effective foundation for the project and set effective and strict implementation system. At micro level, the participation and collaboration of project stakeholders promoted the implementation of the project and achieved preset targets of the projects. The comprehensive poverty reduction joint efforts of many departments and agencies consolidated various resources constrains in normal poverty reduction projects, and a multi-entity participation ensured the poverty reduction measures benefit individual households.

The Southwest Poverty Reduction Project emphasized both the social and economic development and mobilized both the market and government resources. Both the social and economic poverty reduction promoted balanced and comprehensive development which laid foundation for the long term development of the project villages. By mobilizing both the market and government resources, the Government's commitment ensured the progress of the project and the market operation gave dynamic to the project, therefore lead the development of the project regions to a healthy sustainable track.

Major Experiences and Measures Taken in the Project Implementation

The four innovations in the Southwest Poverty Reduction Project are the core of the success experience of the project. The successful experiences and practice in project design, implementation, supervision and management have been widely adopted in other later national poverty production projects.

1. System innovation. As the IFIs for this project, the World Bank introduced scientific management methods and models and provided new theories and ideas for poverty reduction cause in China. The cooperation between the Chinese government and the World Bank had changed the traditional poverty reduction of relying only on domestic capital to create a new cooperation in combining domestic poverty reduction funds with IFI assistance.

2. Organizational innovation. The project has designed a multi-entity participation system. It has changed the traditional one-way participation and defined the rights, responsibilities and benefits of each participating parties more clearly. In addition, this project introduced and established the first Poverty Inspectorate System in China and trained many analysts in poverty inspection and investigation.

3. Technology innovation. There are a total of eight sub-projects under Southwest Poverty Reduction Project. Based on different characteristics of different sub-projects, the World Bank has provided experts and technical assistance which not only introduced new technology with higher productivity, but also trained personnel with new technology.

4. Policy innovation. Southwest Poverty Reduction Project adopted a model of "phased implementation" that effectively increased the input efficiency and mitigated the mismatch and dis-link problems among sub-projects. This model was adopted and disseminated by The National Program for Rural Poverty Reduction and Development (2001 – 2010). In addition, the project paid attention to the gender issue and set strict rules in environment protection which provided experiences for other poverty reduction projects to learn from.

Major Lessons and Problems

The conservative and biased estimation of the change of the external conditions is the major factor that adversely affected the effects of the project. The change in the counterpart funding policy affected the progress of the project. The exchange rate fluctuation resulted in the shrink of the total funding by 14.8%. The change of the domestic and foreign agriculture products market resulted in many adjustment to the original project plan and cancellation of some project components. The institution reform and frequent change of the officials caused breaks in operation management. It not only increased difficulty in training, but also had negative impact on the continuity of the project management.

The implementation of the project should combine with national and cultural situations closely but not too rigid. The components of the projects should be adjusted accordingly with the change of implementation environment to avoid failure in the end. We should emphasis both flexibility and adhering to principle at the same time in the procurement and adjustment procedure. We should take into consideration of the characteristics of some sub-projects themselves in procurement and to avoid losses due to implementation rigidity. We should design a system to improve the local participation based on the cultural situation of the project regions to ensure sustainable effects of the projects.

Source: January 9, 2004, Wu Guobao, A Case Study of China Southwest Poverty Reduction Project.

6.2.5 Knowledge and Institution Development Contribution

Comparing with loans, development knowledge has more significant externalities. If the contribution of assistance loans is local, the effects of policy and knowledge are universal. For instance, IFIs like the World Bank and ADB are not the creditors of loans, but also play very important roles in providing development knowledge. The World Bank Group has many good economists and experts in many sectors and fields, who provide large volume of research funds and accumulated extensive international experiences and knowledge. The research papers they published every year, especially The World Development Report, introduced most recent development in development theory and practice timely, provided in-depth analysis and discussion on major issues related to current and long-term development and constructively raised the ideas for reform and development policies and institution construction. They moved away from providing policy guidance and knowledge and information services for developing countries to provide intangible knowledge, institution and culture. By December 31, 2003, the World Bank had provided 12 technical assistance projects with a total of US$321 million loans (including US$70.4 million hard loan and US$250.6 million soft loans) which was 0.87% of its total loan to China. During the same period of time, ADB has provided 435 technical assistance projects to China with a total loan of US$210 million[①].

Over twenty years ago, the World Bank had started to conduct systematic study over China's economy. It had provided important and positive recommendations to the Chinese Government during different stages in China's reform regarding major issues and challenges that China faced. It had played a role of "Knowledge Bank" of promoting development, namely knowledge innovation, knowledge dissemination, knowledge exchange and knowledge sharing. In 1980, the World Bank published its very first research report *China: Socialist Economic Development* which evaluated the economic development that China achieved during 1949 to 1980, analyzed the major problems in economic and sectoral development in China, and provided several recommendations on China's economic development and economic reform. In 1984, the World Bank published *China: Long-term Development Issues and Plan* which discussed the issues that China might encounter until 2000 and available options. Until recently, the World Bank have published 22 national economic reports, five provincial reports, 74 sector reports, and 75 policy research papers (Table 6.3).

Since 1981, the World Bank has supported Chinese Economic Press to publish every year the Chinese edition of *The World Development Report* every year for over twenty years. These reports reflected the most recent results of development theories, important lessons and experiences of different countries development during different periods of times. Since 1990s, the World Development Report had introduced China's experience in reform and transition many times, such as the *World Development Report 1996*: From Plan to Market, for the first time approved the step by step and adaptive reform approach. *The World Development Report 2000/2001*: Attacking Poverty also appraised the significant contribution that China made to the world poverty reduction. The Chinese Economics Press has published about 195 kinds of World Bank publications that totaled over 860,000 copies. UNDP began to publish *China Human Development Report* since 1995, ADB also submit *China National Economic Report* to the Chinese government regularly to provide macro analysis and development policy recommendations.

---

① Data provided by International Department, Ministry of Finance.

Table 6.3 Statistics on the World Bank group economic research papers in relation to loans to China

Items	Number	Percentage (%)
Economic and sector research	101	47.0
National economy	22	
Provincial economy	5	
Social sector	7	
Education, health and environment	16	
Fiscal, finance, trade	14	
Agriculture, water resources	12	
Industrial, energy	15	
Transportation	10	
Discussion paper	29	14.0
Technical report	1	0.4
Policy research paper	75	35.0
Other publications	7	3.0
Total	213	

Source: July 2002, *the World Bank Group China Operation Overview.*

The development knowledge in these reports have been extensively disseminated among Chinese government and academia and provided important reference for China's economic development and transition. Only during 1994 – 2003, the articles published in Chinese periodicals made nearly 2800 times references to the World Bank publications. On the other hand, the World Bank also helped China develop knowledge economy through Global Development Learning Network and Global Development Gateway. The World Bank Institute conducted training activities using Beijing Global Development Learning Center and had developed courses in Chinese to provide long distance training to the western regions. Connecting Global Development Learning Network with China Education, Science and Research Network make it possible for members to acquire knowledge at very low cost.

The IFIs plays an increasingly important role in providing information and knowledge in relation to development policies. By using their experts and global experts network to these organizations follow up China's economic development systematically, conduct policy analysis, organize consulting activities, make policy recommendations, publish comprehensive report, organize academic seminars, conduct personnel training and long-distance educational trainings, etc. and meet the need for Chinese development and disseminate and share more development knowledge more comprehensively. These knowledge and experiences helped China transit from a planned-economy to a market-based economy step by step and formed a more open integrated domestic market, and established market-based economic institution with Chinese characteristics. Both the Chinese and international experience proved that effective development policy and favorable development environment are more likely to promote economic development and social progress than large volume of international assistance. To a certain extent, IFIs are not only capital providers, but more of providers and disseminators of global development knowledge and experiences to China.

In the meantime, both the World Bank and ADB emphasized state-owned enterprises reform, ownership reform, restructuring, social security system reform, and improve governance in the project design. On the other hand, both the World Bank and ADB are strengthening capacity building of the banking systems to small and medium-sized enterprises all over China to improve the financing channels for these enterprises and provide corporate governance reforms. They supported the restructuring of the state-owned enterprises and the diversification of ownership. In order to support China's finance system reform, the World Bank had published many policy papers that involved state-owned commercial bank restructuring strategy, establishing effective banking supervision system. The World Bank provided technical assistance to the policy bank system construction. Supporting China's financial system reform has been one of the priorities for IFC operation in China. IFC has actively participated in the city bank reform and handling the non-performing loans of the banking system.

Box 6.5 IFI institution building for strengthening public governance

- To assist China to adopt international standard accounting and auditing systems
- To recommend to implement public hearing system to increase public participation and public policy transparency
- To assist Chinese Government in human resource development to train more prosecutors and judges and implement National Qualification Exam for Judges
- To improve consultation system in law drafting and modification and enhance the capacity of the People's Congress in reviewing and approving laws
- To assist Ministry of Finance to introduce far-reaching fiscal system reform, including new procedures for budget preparation
- To implement new budget category and improve supervision and auditing
- To initiate new treasury management system
- To assist the implementation of 2002 Government Procurement Law and 1999 Tendering and Bidding Laws
- To assist China improving statistical methodology and system. China has been participating in the General Data Dissemination System of the International Monetary Fund (IMF)

Source: Asian Development Bank, China Country Strategy and Plan, November 2003.

6.2.6 Sustainable Development Contributions

Both the World Bank and ADB had made ecological issues one of the key areas in their assistance strategies to make efforts to promote China to change from resources predatory development to a resource protective development. As early as 1997, the World Bank published a report entitled *China: Clean Water, Blue Sky* that helped China calculated the human capital loss related to environment pollution.

IFI loan projects are not only focused on expanding productivity, such as expanding water supply and transportation capacity, but emphasized more on improving efficiency through system building. From ADB point of view, their projects are designed to improve efficiency, rather than capacity. The market-based water quality and price system reform supported by ADB had improved economic efficiency, however, ADB did not involved in the strategic reform of the financial sector and the enterprise system reform.

By the end of 2002, ADB had provided US$2.7 billion loans to improve environment, among which about US$2.1 billion loans were used to address "black" pollution problems, and US$600 million loans were used to solve the "green" issues. Total loans for environment related projects are a little less than a quarter of the total ADB loans to China. ADB also provided 119 environment related technical assistance with total of US$77 million funds.

Through technical assistance, ADB played important strategic roles in setting China's environment related policy and legal framework and improving environmental evaluation. In the meantime, it provided loans to address city environment pollution and waste disposal directly.

Improving environment related laws and policy supervision: In order to build up capacity, ADB provided assistance in personnel training. It also assisted in amendments to the Water Pollution Prevention and Control Act (1996), draft of Land Administration Law (1998), and the draft of Clean Production Promotion Law (2002). ADB supported the evaluation of environmental protection basic law and the establishment of natural resources legislation framework.

Developing market mechanism: the study supported by ADB on implementing waste discharge fee system and SO_2 emission trade helped China seek opportunities in reducing greenhouse gas emission and preventing global warming. With the help off ADB, China has started to implement the national city-water price management rules. The new city water price system was based on the principle of complete recovering of cost, and also taken into consideration of preserving water, payment capacity of the poor and the public opinions.

Capacity building of environment related key institutions: In order to strengthen environment management capacity, ADB had provided technical assistance to State Environmental Protection Administration and local environmental protection bureaus of eleven cities and one province to develop environmental protection plans, promote capacity building for environment assessment, and abiding by the rules and regulations of environmental protections.

References

[1] Jin Liqun. Introduction, Economic Development: Theories and Practices. Beijing: Economic Science Press, 2002. p.26

[2] Nicholas Stern.,2002. Preface, Economic Development: Theories and Practices. Beijing: Economic Science Press, 2002. p.4

[3] ADB. Evaluation on China's country strategy, translated by the post evaluation dept of China International Engineering Consultation Corp, Dec. 1998. p.19

7 Experiences of IFI Operations

The success of a country's development depends on both the external and internal factors. International assistance will help a country's development, however, the deciding factor for a country's development are the internal factors, namely whether the development strategy is successful, whether the development targets are appropriate, whether the development policies are correct and whether the development capacities have been improved. In China's case, the external and internal factors are combined effectively. With a relatively low level of assistance received, China has maximized the development achievement.

Over twenty years ago, IFIs provided timely help to China. The IFI loans not only helped China opened the door to the outside world, but also brought with them capital, technology, equipment and management experiences and became major sources for China to acquire, learn and absorb market economy and development policies. They also had extensive influences over system arrangement, viewpoint innovation and development of knowledge and technology. Meanwhile, they integrated China into the world. They objectively introduced the development achievement of China to the world, and shared China's development experiences with other developing countries. This is a major driving force for China's opening to the outside world and is the greatest contribution that IFI loans had made which is far greater than loans themselves. Over the past two decades, the annual project loan inflow to China has been US$5 billion, which accounted for less than 1% of China's GDP. In comparison, the annual FDI inflow exceeded US$50 billion. This showed that the investment climate improved dramatically, and the market capacity of attracting private investment has been increased substantially.

During the project construction and operation, the Chinese government and IFIs had established good cooperation inter-relationship of helping, exchanging and inter-learning. IFIs had provided China with reform, economic construction and project management experiences from other developing and transitional countries. They praised the great achievements that Chinese government had achieved, in the meantime, identified the issues and challenges during difference stages of economic development in China and provided large amount of lessons and experiences for China to learn from during China's economic reform. In the process of reform and opening to the outside world, China had combined with local situations, creatively achieved economic development and economic reform, as Nicolas Stern had once put it that the World Bank had made efforts to introduce China's success experiences to other developing countries and made the whole world benefits from China's experiences[1]. IFI loans are not "free lunch", they are not the "blood transfusion machines" either. In order to make international assistance a success, the development capacity of the recipient country must be strengthened and develop "blood making function" and lay foundation for sustainable development. These are the successful experiences that China can offer.

7.1 The Greatest Success is the Success of Development Strategy, from a Pro-Economic Growth Development to a Development Viewpoint of People First

The development strategy of a country is very important to its development path and achievements. The success of strategy is the greatest success; on the contrary, the mistake of development strategy is the biggest mistake. Successful development depends on continuing learning, accumulation and innovation of development strategy practice, correct judgment of local situations of the country, a careful design of development strategy, pro-active approaches in addressing development challenges, and flexible adjustment to the development policies. China's development strategy had changed from pro-economic growth development to a development strategy of people first.

In 1999, the World Bank developed Comprehensive Development Framework for 21st century. The World Bank's priorities are outlined in the Strategic Directions Paper under two groups: the Corporate Advocacy Priorities (CAPs①) and the Global Public Goods Priorities (GPGPs). GAPs focused on investment climate, public governance, education and health, while GPGPs included communicable disease control, environmental issues, trade and integration, information and knowledge, and international financial framework. The long-term strategy of ADB focused on sustainable economic growth, comprehensive social development, better rule of law, private sector development, regional cooperation, and environmental sustainability. Its country assistance strategy emphasized on promoting equal and balanced growth, improving market operation mechanism, promoting regional cooperation and environmental sustainability. (see Table 8.2)

Entered into 21st century, the major challenges that China faced are how to maintain a sustainable, equal development and reduce poverty and regional disparities and promote comprehensive human development. The development

① CAPs are defined as the "the critical enablers of poverty reduction that the Bank is particularly well-qualified to champion by sharing knowledge (both research and experience) and building awareness with clients, development partners, and other stakeholders". They build on two key pillars of the Strategic framework paper (a) building the climate for investment, jobs and sustainable growth and (b) empowering poor people to participate in development and investing in them.

targets are not only focused on economic growth, but more on the purpose of economic growth, namely to meet the growing material and cultural needs of over 1 billion population, therefore, to achieve higher level of human development, and enjoy higher level of quality of living and public services. The experience of SARS made the Chinese government realized that growth is only a means to development; the objective of the development is to improve the living standard and quality of people, and the health and life of the people and level of human development. Recently the Chinese government raised a new development viewpoint of people first, and further emphasized the new development principles of "five balanced aspects", namely balancing urban and rural development, balancing development among regions, balancing economic and social development, balancing development of man and nature, and balancing domestic development and opening wider to the outside world (2004, Wen Jiabao), thus formulated the second generation of development strategy that targeted a coordinated, comprehensive and sustainable development. This new strategy will mitigate social conflicts and ensure China a sustainable development and lay a foundation for long-term harmony between human and nature.

7.2 Enhancing the Relationship and Compatibility between the IFI Assistance Strategy and Development Targets of Chinese Government

During the past twenty years, China had experienced different stages in economic development, and confronted with different challenges during different stages, thus had different development strategies and focuses. In this process, the World Bank and ADB understood the development targets, strategies and policies of the Chinese government during different economic development stages and took the initiative to cooperate with the Chinese government with compatible country assistance strategy. Take ADB for an example, the assistance targets in 1991 was to improve economic operation efficiency, reduce poverty, and protect environment and natural resources. In 1997, poverty reduction targets were adjusted to be achieved through accelerating economic growth of inland provinces and reduce poverty population. By 2002, ADB no longer provided loans for financial, commercial (such as industry, agro-industry, agro-processing) and some infrastructure sectors (such as ports and communication). ADB changed to pro-poor economic development, and committed to create private sector development friendly environment, strengthen public governance, promote regional cooperation that will assist China in further integrating into the world economy and promote environmental sustainability. It emphasized more on coordinated, equal and sustainable development. Entered into the latter part of 1990's, the urbanization process accelerated, the state-owned enterprises reform and laid-off workers had created an ever deteriorating incidence of urban poverty.

Both the World Bank and ADB implemented poverty reduction plan through many technical assistance projects that targeting urban poverty population. They also made policy recommendations to promote a more equal development in regard to the development inequality between the rich coastal provinces and poor inland provinces and income inequality between rural and urban population[2].

Development assistance will not necessarily promote the development of recipient countries which largely depends on the internal development factors. From the international assistance experience of various countries it can be found that the faster a country's economy grows the greater supporting or promoting roles that development assistance will play. The recipient will benefit from both the supply factor of supporting growth and the demand factor of stimulating growth. On the one hand, assistance can improve investment climate and infrastructure, promote human resources development and improve skills and quality of labors. On the other hand, the stronger a country's structural policy capability, the greater role the assistance will play. Therefore, reform and structural policy of a country will form complementary relationship with development assistance.

The funding assistance from IFIs can only be effective under a good policy environment. If an economy is engaged in reform, IFIs can provide key support through policy recommendations, trainings and capital support, therefore, the improved economic system and progress of policies of the recipient countries are the key factors for assistance capital to promote the development of recipient countries. As a large but less developed continent, Africa had received the most international assistance. However, the overall development effects have always been unsatisfactory. On the contrary, Asia is a place that gave birth to miracles. A good policy climate, and IFI assistance strategy that is compatible with national development strategy are much more effective than tens of millions of capital support in promoting development. Thus, to some extent, China is a successful model for close combination of international development assistance and targets.

An ADB evaluation report over China operation concluded that both the central and local governments have been making efforts to raise domestic counterpart funds for ADB bank loans and establish appropriate matching system, which showed very strong sense of ownership to the projects[3]. Various new system arrangements brought into China with IFI loans have played greater roles in the reform and opening to the outside world and brought in bigger direct benefits that are far greater than IFI loans. Take highway development in China for example, IFI loans only accounted for a small proportion of the total investment, however, it successfully introduced in the toll system and made China a country with the second longest highway system (Box 7.1). Multilateral development agencies, such as the World Bank transferred development ideas and development experiences to developing countries. They are also the disseminators of knowledge and experiences; they are the propeller to the economic development.

Box 7.1 Leveraging Private Capital from Existing Toll Roads in China

The total highway mileage in China was only 700 kilometers in 1992. In 2003, the total mileage exceeded 30,000 kilometers and China became the country with the second longest highway system in the world following United States of America. During the 1990s, China's demand for capital to finance its highway program triggered an estimated US$12 billion in new highway capital from private sources, without sovereign guarantees. This represented about 10 percent of total investment in the road sector. Private capital flows peaked in 1996 – 1997 then steeply dropped in the wake of the Asian financial crisis. However, private investors are showing renewed interest in road projects.

Investment came in the form of equity from Hong Kong and the domestic markets as well as creative use of existing toll highways and bridges, including World Bank-funded assets, to leverage new private finance. During the 1990s, 20 such asset securitization transactions were completed with the issuance of shares to foreign or domestic investors. Total capital raised from these listing exceeds US$2 billion. The World Bank participated in five separate transactions which helped pioneer this approach, in which operating road and bridge assets that it had earlier financed were injected into the balance sheets of newly-listed provincial expressway development companies for shares listing on the Hong Kong and Shenzhen stock exchanges. The proceeds were used to build or expand additional expressways in the province. The IFIs' reputation and assets have contributed greatly to the initial creditworthiness of the listed development companies, and very likely given an added level of comfort to investors as well.

Source: *China Country Assistance Strategy* (2003 – 2005), World Bank Group, January, 2003.

7.3 As a Recipient, China Should Sit in the Driver's Seat and all the Assistance Activities Should Serve the Needs of China

Getting IFI loans is not the purpose for the cooperation between the Chinese government and IFIs but a major means to promote China's opening to the outside world and development. The purpose of further strengthening cooperation is not to get more assistance but to make the project genuinely benefit the people. As recipient country, Chinese government insisted on sitting in the driver's seat and made all the assistance activities serve Chinese government: to learn from international development theory and experiences rather than imitate indiscriminately; to learn rather than follow blindly; to innovate rather than copy. China has played dominate role in deciding the source of the projects, designing in the project, and execution of the project. Thus the projects are to serve the development strategy and plan of the Chinese government. This is a domestic demand and self-development-lead tactic in absorbing and utilizing international development assistance.

In fact, since the latter part of 1990's, official development assistance accounted for less than 1.5% of total government expenditure [4]. While the percentage of fiscal revenue in GDP increased from 11% in 1995 to 18.5% in 2002. In addition, the total transfer payment from central government to local governments (mainly inland poor regions) increased by six times[①]. From 1998 to 2003, the Chinese government adopted proactive fiscal policy to stimulate domestic demand and issued a total of RMB 800 billion treasury bond to support largely infrastructure construction that would benefit the long-term development. Both the international and Chinese experiences show that any IFIs development assistance or projects must conform to domestic situation and decided by the recipient country based on actual situations. In addition, the government should encourage local residents, private enterprises and NGO, especially the poor, to participate and support the projects and make recipient regions and targeted people really benefit from the projects. The key is to improve domestic project management capacity (Box 7.2). Since 1980s, there are five categories and total of 89 national and ministerial documents in relation to IFI loan project management have been promulgated (namely comprehensive management, project financial management, debt management, procurement and bidding management, and others) [5].

Box 7.2 How does the Chinese government to strengthen project management capability?

(1) Initial selection of projects to ensure that the projects are aligned with government priorities;

(2) Clear allocation of responsibility at the executing agency level to plan and implement projects and to mobilize substantial counterpart funding before a decision is made to borrow;

(3) Feasibility studies prepared by the executing agency, which are independently checked by central government agencies with further quality enhancement through project preparatory technical assistance (PPTA) work, especially in the areas of financial and economic analysis, and resettlement planning;

(4) A requirement for local environmental protection bureaus to sign off on domestically prepared environmental impact assessments;

① During this period, the public spending in education, health and science and technology increased 230%, social security spending increased 950%, and agriculture spending increased 190%.

(5) The establishment of executing agencies that are adequately staffed by competent professionals who are involved in project preparation, before external development funds are made available.

Source: Asian Development Bank, *China Country Strategy and Plan* (2004 – 2006), November 2003.

7.4 Institution Building and Institution Innovation in Project Management

7.4.1 Capacity Building

IFIs emphasize on the cross-sector capacity building through projects, especially strengthening the comprehensive capacity building of human capital and sustainable development.

In order to solve social problems, the World Bank Group provided assistance and support to social security analysis and capacity building. The IFC TA focused on capacity building, while the loan assistance to the western regions were mainly used in financial sector capacity building, investment climate building for private sector development, corporate governance, and participation of private sector in infrastructure services. IFC projects targeted to strengthen small and medium-sized enterprises (SME) capacity building and develop alternative sources for SME financing and the capacity of local banking system lending to SME.

ADB supported TA projects that targeted the capacity building of multi-project implementation agencies. ADB will use knowledge products to promote market-based enforcement and support capacity building of local administrative agencies; strengthen poverty impacts to broaden the coverage and improve institutional capacity and administrative efficiency of the social safety net; build capacity for the management of regional cooperation, regional economic surveillance, and regional aspects of the new international financial infrastructure.

7.4.2 Institution Building

IFIs attached importance to establish effective management mechanism and institution to assist the efficient operation of the projects; to develop a set of performance indicators to strengthen monitoring and supervision and evaluate the project; and to set up project data bank as the base for knowledge dissemination. In the project life cycle, ADB attached great importance to the project management and performance tracking. This practice has been concluded in ADB's project operation evaluation as one of the importance experience for China to become the best-performing portfolio of any large country in the ADB (Box 7.3).

Box 7.3 ADB main lessons learned from China's project evaluation

- The impacts of major policy changes in transition economies (e.g., trade and price liberalization, greater competition and reliance on market forces, financial sector and exchange rate regime changes) on any particular project is difficult to predict, thus increasing project risk.
- Well-conceived implementation arrangements, and adequate assistance from the ADB, particularly during project implementation, are essential for effective project completion.
- There is a need to provide training related to ADB operations and to develop sector country knowledge before lending.
- Environmental mitigation measures and compliance with environmental standards need to be carefully monitored during implementation and after project completion.
- More effort is needed to develop verifiable, monitorable indicators and to quantify baseline conditions to provide a better basis for measuring project impacts on improving socioeconomic conditions and reducing poverty.
- Project design should include interventions to strengthen capacity particularly in inland provinces.
- In some cases the quantity and quality of Asian Development Bank review missions need to be improved.

Source: Asian Development Bank, *Country assistance strategy and plan* (2004 – 2006), November 2003.

The China Country Strategy of the World Bank was designed to identify special issues that will increase risks or have adverse effects on the quality of the projects. Many of the problems have been identified in previous evaluation of the World Bank Operation Evaluation Department, Quality Assurance Committee, and Annual Operation Evaluation and various regional and departmental sector evaluations (among the problems previously identified, many of them are in relation to simplify and speed up project preparation, procurement and disbursement procedures. These recommendations have been implemented in the procedure simplification and management decentralization during FY 1998). Cross-sector problems were to be resolved through special inspection or evaluation, and dialogue with relevant departments or local governments.

7.4.3 Learning Capacity Building

IFIs helped recipient countries to effectively make use of global knowledge resources and increase the externalities of technical assistance and institution innovation. IFC has been working to establish Global Development Learning Network (GDLN) and Global Development Gateway.

A significant characteristic of the World Bank Knowledge Agenda is the closer integration of economic and sector tasks containing a high operational content with capacity building conducted through World Bank Institute, and trust funds and research on strategic issues undertaken by the World Bank in collaboration with local and international researchers and institutions. Notably, some major economic and sector studies are carried out with the World Bank Institute courses, including use of Global Development Learning Network programs, in order to transfer cutting-edge analytical methods or international experience to local counterparts, or to disseminate findings more broadly. Through this way, the World Bank Group can bring longer-term development problems to the Chinese government's attention and conduct leading researches while also assisting policymakers to deal with the more immediate economic and social agenda.

The Asian Development Bank Institute (ADBI) is also an important source of knowledge-based products and its work will be better used to provide an analytical basis for ADB's policy dialogue. Strengthening the impact of knowledge products should not be limited to advisory technical assistance operations. Institutional reform associated with ADB loans and policy dialogue during project design and implementation also provide opportunities to introduce best international practice and strengthen the policy impact of ADB operations. Mechanisms need to be developed to better disseminate the findings and lessons learned from ADB's operation experience in China (including findings of evaluation studies) and the efficacy of knowledge products to senior Chinese leaders, private sectors, and academia. The terms of reference and budgets for every advisory technical assistance operation and sector study should provide for a dissemination strategy.

7.4.4 Balance between Productivity and Efficiency

IFI loan programs are largely designed to be development, strategy and policy-oriented. They are intended to improve the development capacity of the recipient countries through technical assistance and advisory consulting rather than just build up a physical project. They are not only designed to enhance productivity, but also to improve project implementation efficiency through institution building.

The nature of the World Bank lending relationship with China has always been based on support for agreed sector policy objectives. Operations were to reflect the clients' strong ownership and reform objectives developed to bring about significant and sustained reform progress rather than simply enhance productivity. Consistency with sectoral strategies and potential for innovation/

knowledge transfer formed the criteria for project selection. In project design and implementation, the World Bank continually looked for opportunities to transfer new approaches and technologies. Each project was designed to build on the earlier lessons and when situation is appropriate to introduce innovation as part of project selection and design.

As far as Asian Development Bank is concerned, projects were designed to improve efficiency rather than enhance productivity only. The water quality and water price reform to promote market-based operation supported by the Asian Development Bank improved economic efficiency. In the financial sector, ADB supported investment funds for small and medium-sized enterprises (SMEs), the environment, and instruments to address non-performing loans. ADB took measures to expand its lending to public sector to assist the private sector development and promote innovation in the cooperation between the government and private sectors in road, railroad, energy and water resources management.

References

[1] Nicholas Stern, 2002. Preface, Jin Liqun, Nicholas Stern. Economic Development: Theory and Practice. Beijing: Economic Science Press, p.4

[2] World Bank. Promoting the Equitable Growth, Chinese Version. Beijing: Tsinghua University Press, 2004

[3] ADB. China Country Strategy and Program (2004 – 2006), November 2003

[4] ADB. China Country Strategy and Program (2004 – 2006), November 2003

[5] International Department. MOF: Collection of Documents on IFI Loans Management. Beijing: China Financial and Economic Press, 2001

8 Issues and Policy Recommendations

8.1 Issues

1. Insufficient understanding of costs, benefits and related risks associated with some of the projects

At the beginning of reform and opening to the outside world, China did not have sufficient construction capital and foreign reserve. In order to improve infrastructure and improve the living standard of the people, various levels of governments actively attracted IFI loans of all kinds① to support projects including rural healthcare and water supply projects. These projects have very strong externalities associated with public goods and were very weak in terms of withstanding risks. Therefore, to sustain various service activities with only the returns from the projects is very difficult. Such projects do not have sustainability, thus require sustainable input and support of public finance. Therefore, when applying for loans for public service type of projects, the government needs to consider repayment capability prudently to avoid increasing financial burden for itself. In addition, a standard transfer payment system can be established in the process. Different levels of government, in addition to raise counterpart funds, need to share the loan repayment as well.

IFI loans are not grants. They need to be repaid with principle and interest. Because some projects have a long project cycle, there are interest and exchange risks. During project design and operation, some local governments did not make correct judgment on self-development, comprehensive fiscal capacity, and out-of-control risks and irresistible force associated with projects, did not establish an effective loan repayment mechanism and timetable. For some poor provinces, the annual interest payment accounted for a significant proportion of the local fiscal revenue. Therefore, loan repayment brought great pressure on the local finance. They can only rob Peter to pay Paul or request transfer payment from higher level of government to repay debt. This directly increased the credit risk of the government.

2. Insufficient analysis under or over estimate of project benefits and extremely long project cycle expose the projects to policy and exchange risks

For some projects, from projects preparation, feasibility study to the final

① It is not excluded that the local government using loans as resources they can allocate which creates possible rent-seeking.

commencement, it could take several or even tens of years. Because the construction cycle is very long, the results and evaluations of the projects are quite different from the expected results set during project preparation. To certain extend, this reflects the defect in project design. In the meantime, the international and domestic economic and political climates kept changing dynamically, various policies also changed, such as rise of prices, exchange rate and interest rate adjustment, will all affect the development of project. In addition, personnel change in project management and execution agencies also broke the continuity of project construction. Thus the long approval and construction cycles expose the project to policy, market and management risks, which are not in favor of the development of the projects, and added pressure on the future debt repayment of the project entities.

3. Lack of management and coordination among responsible agencies related to loan projects

Many of the IFI projects are comprehensive development projects, every project from application, project selection, implementation, loan repayment, and sustainable development, there are many related agencies involved at different levels. These agencies are responsible for project management, supervision and implementation. Thus there is not a clear definition of responsibilities among different agencies in the project design, feasibility study phases and processes. The defects in management mechanism such as organization, planning, responsibility, control, supervision, and incentive lead to inappropriate coordination among project responsible agencies and entities. The problems in coordination and management, such as investors are not policy makers, legal person is responsible for project management, etc. There are unsatisfactory cases in equipment procurement, financial management, cost control and profit models.

First of all, the equipment procurement procedure is not flexible enough, while disbursement procedure is too complicated. For some projects, it took two or three years from submitting procurement plan to the actual installation of the equipment. However, equipment, especially electronics like computers, is updated very rapidly. Equipment was the new models when submitted in the plan, but when it actually got to the projects, it was already out of date and could not meet the needs of the market thus could not be used and resulted in waste of funds.

On the other hand, the complexity of the procurement method delayed the procurement progress. According the rules of IFIs, different procurement methods applied to different size of procurement contracts: international bidding must be used for a procurement contract over US$500,000, while shopping is for contract under US$500,000. Many projects are large, and most of the procurement packages are above US$500,000. To follow through the complex procurement procedure would definitely delay the procurement process, and the US$500,000 procurement limit can not meet the need of the project with the increase of price.

In addition, the disbursement procedure is very complex. The letter of commitment is the major disbursement approach used by ADB loans while direct payment and special account methods are less used. The above factors affected the efficiency of the project implementation. Besides, the Chinese administrative institutions (especially the Ministry of Finance) have not established a complete and accurate project database, the follow-up investigation and evaluation cannot be conducted regularly.

4. The financial management should get improved some project entities violated the financial rules and loan agreements

Loan management can be categorized into two types: one is the direct management of project loans, and the other one is the management of counterpart funds of the projects. In the first case, several issues were found including ambiguous division of responsibilities and functions among various institutions, loose monitoring system to evaluate the implementation and the project objectives, no responsibility management sense and related regulations, loan funds were used for other purposes, not-honored commitment in counterpart funds in some grass-roots project entities. The provision of counterpart funds depended heavily on the counties in some projects, because of the constrains resulted from the under-development of local economy, the unrealized local counterpart funds seriously affected the effectiveness of the projects. All these issues are good examples for illustrating the shortcomings of the Chinese investment and financing system, and the current loan management system.

According to the information provided by the State Audit Administration and the Ministry of Finance, some provinces, sectors and project entities attached greater importance to project numbers and amounts of loans rather than project quality and management; some project entities violated the financial rules and regulations and even the loan agreements, some loan management institutions shortened the on-lending terms, added interest spreads and management fees, made false statement to get the loans funds, changed project materials for profit, counterpart funds were not provided as agreed. Some projects had low investment returns, poor loan repayment capabilities and provided false financial statements. Some local and sector governments interfered the independent rights of audit departments to protect local and sector interests which placed barriers for the punishment and disclosure to the IFIs[1]. Regarding the above issues, the State Audit Administration and the Ministry of Finance issued an official document in 1999 to strengthen the auditing and monitoring work for the projects financed by IFIs.

5. Weak project post evaluation and the sustainability of the projects needs further strengthening

The post-evaluation on the IFI loan projects are generally not enough. This shows that the overall post-evaluation capacity of the Chinese government is not strong. To improve post-evaluation work will significantly sustain continuous attention of IFIs, government and project entities to the projects, thus ensure the sustainable effects of the projects. In addition, improved post-evaluation will summarize experience and lessons scientifically and effectively to set up the base for guiding future projects and improve the cooperation between the recipient countries and IFIs.

8.2 Policy Recommendations

1. China still needs to secure more loans from ifis and ensure efficient use of the loans in the future

(1) There is great regional disparity in China, about 2/3 of the regions still need loans from IFIs

Based on the current level of per capita GDP, it is very likely that China will "graduate" from development assistance of the IFIs in the next five years. However, one single indicator of per capita GDP can not reflect the real economic situation in China. The regional disparity in China is so huge that it could be described as "one China, four worlds". At present, most of the areas in central and western part of China belong to the Fourth World (not including Heilongjiang and Jilin). This means 630 million people live in lower income areas, which accounts for half of the total population. This is one important basis for China to use more loans from IFIs.

Generally speaking, the percentage of central government fiscal expenditure in GDP is pretty low (only 3% – 4%), therefore, it is a challenge for the government to provide basic public services for 1.3 billion people, especially for 630 million people who live in the lower income areas. We still need assistance and support from IFIs in poverty reduction, environment protection and rural infrastructure construction, etc. There are still much to be accomplished for IFIs loans in the vast central and western part of China and rural areas.

(2) The transfer payment of central government to local governments and the assistance fund should be packaged with loans from IFIs to provide timely help to the local development and improve efficiency

Based on the development experience of the past two decades, central government grants packaged with IFI loans can play very positive roles in promoting development in less developed regions and the development of public service sectors. IFIs have served as "knowledge bank" in many occasions rather than a simple loan institute. To work closely with them, China can get not only loans but also knowledge and technologies in relation to development, therefore can improve the efficiency and effectiveness of funds. The development experiences of Thailand and Malaysia show that the development level and capacities were reduced and affected after assistance loans stopped. In fact, the relationship between the IFIs and recipient countries is not just a relationship of borrowers and lenders, but "development, cooperation, mutual-beneficiary and win-win for all parties".

(3) To use IFI loans in mixed private/public ownership sectors will improve the efficiency of using global resources in China

Those competitive sectors with high long-term returns, such as power generation, higher education, commercial pension and insurance, health insurance, life insurance, private health services, non-basic health, city water supply, water treatment, etc., still need loans from IFIs as "seed money" to promote the sector policy. Although loans to these sectors only accounted for very small portion of the total loan, the participation of IFIs facilitated the use of global resources and contributed to foreign private investment in these sectors. Therefore, in the future China still needs to actively get IFIs involved in these sectors.

2. To actively explore new ways of international cooperation and share the development achievements with the rest of the developing world

The government should coordinate its international cooperation with IFIs among internal institutions and organizations. Traditionally, the government tended to allocate projects among IFIs based on regional specialization, project size and the complexity of the projects, leaving IFIs to work on different geographical areas and sector issues. At the present, the coordination function of the Chinese government is split among various ministries and organizations. For instance, Ministry of Finance is responsible for loan and selected grant assistance, and the Ministry of Commerce is responsible for bilateral grants. These projects are different and inter-related which require extensive coordination among these international assistance agencies to reduce duplication in certain areas and focus on helping China to achieve "Millennium Development Goals".

The comparative advantages of China's partners should be effectively capitalized and the knowledge and experience be shared to improve the efficiency of assistance projects and help China to address the complex challenges. It is also necessary to encourage donors and other partners to share knowledge and collaborate, such as encouraging the World Bank to seek co-financing with bilateral donors to soften the overall financing package for social sector and poverty reduction projects, to improve their effectiveness by building on complementary interests and capacities.

It is also encouraged to innovate more effective and diverse financing models, such as the cofinancing by the EU, the World Bank and GEF to support Sustainable Forestry Project, and Australian Agency for International Development (AusAID) provided grant built a distance learning center in the poor western province of Ningxia, for which the World Bank is the project implementing agency. These collaborations made good use of the comparative advantages of each donor, were very effective, and highly appraised by the government.

The government should support the international cooperation among IFIs, domestic NGOs, and civil society groups. With the transit from "political ruling" to "social ruling" in the future, the civil society groups will play an increasingly important role in China's development. To cooperate with NGOs will become a new way of cooperation for IFIs. The World Bank has assisted them in various ways, namely through the Small Grants Program, which for instance awarded a grant to the Women's Federation in Xishuangbanna Dai Nationality Autonomous Prefecture in Yunnan province, where HIV/AIDS infection rates have been increasing dramatically to finance a series of workshops on AIDS prevention and control. Local NGOs have been involved in some World Bank-supported projects implementation, for instance the local women's federation is part of the steering committee of the Anning Valley Development Project and played a leading role in mobilizing local women to participate in project activities and providing training for poor women. In view of this, the government has changed from restricting the involvement of local NGOs in international cooperation to encouraging their participation and guiding the local NGOs to play a positive role in achieving the overall development goals.

With accession to the WTO in December 2001, a process that will largely be completed by 2007, the Chinese government has made extensive commitments to further liberalize entry into economic activities and speed up reforms. In some cases, the direction of changes in the economy is foreseeable. In order to achieve successful adjustment to such changes, the on-going policy reforms need to be intensified, such as mobilizing market-based instruments for macroeconomic management, resolving banking system distress, and trade and investment policy reform. In others, new institutions are required to improve the investment climate, and to promote the functioning of broader, deeper and more dynamic markets for stable and sustained economic growth. These include legal and judicial institution, policies that encouraging competition and supporting private sector development, proved corporate governance, and better provision of public services. The Chinese government should initiate more cooperation with IFIs to help China honor the commitments made in the accession agreement and complete the accession process successfully.

3. To promote the transition from assistance to market guidance

The key to sustain economic and employment growth in the future lies less in factor accumulation but more in economy-wide growth in productivity. The Chinese financial institutions and enterprises need to be more competitive and viable in order to achieve this goal. In market competition and market mechanism, China should make good use of various advantages of IFIs to achieve the transition from assistance to market.

The recent Bank Group Private Sector Strategy will assist this process. Major aims of the Strategy is to (1) help deepen and broaden the financial sector and support the growth of private financial institutions; (2) support industrial restructuring and ownership diversification; (3) improve the business environment by assisting government's efforts in building legal and institutional foundation of market economy; (4) support the adoption and dissemination of environmentally and socially responsible and sustainable business practices by the Chinese private sector; and (5) promote private sector participation in social and physical infrastructure services. Towards these ends, the Chinese government should adopt the following measures: (1) to use International Financial Corporation (IFC) to facilitate and provide services to private enterprises entering the above mentioned sectors; (2) to provide knowledge and experience to private enterprises and financial institutions in using loans of IFIs; (3) to gradually increase the capacities of non-government sector (mainly enterprises and financial institutions) in using IFIs and helping Chinese enterprises "going out of the country".

4. The allocation of ifis loans should conform to the public investment structure of various provinces and regions and requirements should be differentiated based on the public investment level of different sectors and regions, increase investment to the central and western part of china

The public investment transition has largely completed after two decades of reform. The IFI loans should be changed from assisting public investment transition to promoting public investment. The loans should promote public finance investment in public sectors, such as health, education, social security, environment protection, etc., rather than substitute government investment in these sectors, especially in the eastern part of China. However, in the central and western part of China where government funding is insufficient, IFIs can increase the percentage of investment in semi-public sectors, such as roads and energy.

In public sectors such as education, environment protection, public health and rural water supply, etc., IFIs should require the local government to increase their public investment level. As for semi-public sectors and non-public sectors (such as energy and transportation), such restrictions should not be applied to projects in the less developed central and western regions. Meanwhile, IFIs should reduce their investment in the semi-public sectors in eastern regions.

IFI loans should be focused on central and western regions to improve the much needed basic infrastructure, economic infrastructure, policy environment where FDI is less likely to invest compared with the eastern part of China. In central and western part of China, most of the IFI loans are invested in the non-productive sectors that are not capable to improve local investment climate given the long project cycle, such as agriculture, health, education and environment sectors whose capability in providing counterpart funding are relatively weak. IFIs should increase their investment in infrastructure sectors, such as transportation, energy, water resources, to attract more foreign private investment. Central government should implement favorable policies for the utilization of IFI loans in central and western part of China.

5. Enhance project management to implement an "investor responsible system"

Financial management is the core of project management, which directly affects the outcome of the projects and reflects the implementation capabilities. Effective disbursement in the projects depends on the finance mechanism of the related department and entities. The issues related to the debt repayment and disbursement will be resolved if China can provide macro and micro coordination in investment and finance and establish a project implementation system to ensure the implementation of the IFIs lending projects.

The investment system reform should be deepened to establish an "investor responsible system", i.e. whoever make the investment will be responsible for setting up the project, making related decisions, and repaying loans. In fact, many of the issues in loan projects are closely related to the fiscal system and investment system in the process of reform. The core of effective use of IFI loans is whether the loans are repaid in time. However, in the investment system the 'investor' has long missed when one institute repays the debt, while another institute makes investment decisions. As a result, the break in the link between project selection and debt repayment lead to debt repayment problems in some projects. In the investment system reform in the future, the legal person or responsible entity status of the "investor" should be further clarified. "Investor" should be the entity that assumes full responsibilities in project selection, construction, management and supervision process to provide an effective system to ensure the success of the projects.

6. Further improve various systems and mechanisms in relation to IFI loans

Making use of the IFI loans is not only a flow management of financing, utilizing, generating returns and debt repaying, but also a process to learn from the standard practice of the international financial process to establish systems and mechanisms such as project selection system, management mechanism, supervision mechanism and demonstration mechanism.

In order to implement the project successfully, achieve all the targets set during the project preparation and meet the requirement of debt repayment, the capabilities of project application entities in feasibility studies was recommended to be improved to enhance the systems of project evaluation and approval entities and reasonable participation of various government agencies in the project selection and interference, to improve project evaluation work and select more projects with high value return and high success possibilities through establishing and improving project selection system and win higher reputation.

The success of IFI loan projects largely depends on the management level during the project cycle. During project execution, the overall management level needs to be improved in order to sustain an effective progress and development speed and achieve expected results, while reinvestment and increased cost that had to made to improve project execution can be avoided. It is recommended that a system be established to reserve knowledge and high quality personnel. It is also recommended that a more rational organizational establishment and scientific distribution of responsibilities (drawing in from international practice, investors should participate or replace legal person in the management and promote the reform of project governance), establishment of matching incentives, strengthen control and execution capacity, improve the coordination between risks and planning (scientific planning and strategy may avert or mitigate risks), and establish a risk management mechanism, set up a coordinative management system of different level of responsible entities and government agencies and improve project execution capacity. The management capability is a guarantee for the success of the projects. Measures need to be taken to coordinate different levels of management of various project entities to increase the ability of the project to withstand risks, and lay a good foundation for the project.

At present, government-lead-loan is the major form of IFI loans to China. The government has the responsibility to assist and promote the establishment of a third-party supervisory mechanism of different level and different stages. Establishing case bank, post-evaluate system (such as setting up national evaluation bureau), introduce specialized evaluation institute and experts to participate in drafting and improving sector and evaluation standard system. Establishing responsibility tracking system that will enable us to identify and address the problems dynamically during and after the implementation of the projects. This will strengthen the creditworthiness of related agencies at various levels which will also maintain the international reputation of Chinese projects, so that credit crisis will be effectively eliminated.

The cooperative framework with the IFIs has been established through lending operations in the past dozen years. As a recipient country, the lessons and experiences of the past practices should be summarized. It has significant impact to disseminate the advanced theories and results in implementing the projects to other projects. The experiences should also be taken by various assistance projects. To screen and disseminate the demonstration projects is an efficient approach to improve the success rate, effectiveness, rate of return and sustainability of other projects which will strengthen the confidence of various parties and promote the internal development and international cooperation as well.

7. Actively conduct international cooperation, explore new ways of international cooperation with IFI in the new era

In recent years, the IFI loan to China has been declining dramatically. At the same time, the relationship between IFIs and China has undergone a significant change and entered a new era, from one-way relationship of assisting agency and recipient country to a relationship of mutual cooperation and mutual beneficiary. In this context, China should make a role change from a recipient to an assistance giver and actively support the economic development of other developing countries. In the past twenty years, China had successfully solved all the major development issues that any developing country might face. Thus, it is very important that China would introduce and disseminate its development experience, especially technology advancement, policy options, human resources development, system building and innovation, to other developing countries and make knowledge contribution in other developing countries development in economic growth, structure transition, social development and sustainable development.

In the future, China should increase comprehensive international cooperation through (1) encouraging investment of Chinese enterprises in developing countries① [2], such as providing export credits to domestic enterprises to encourage exporting high-tech, resources exploration, and infrastructure construction, etc.; (2) further increasing government assistance to other developing countries with all kinds of development assistance or loans with favorable terms; (3) sharing our development experiences with other developing countries; (4) cooperating with developing countries in social environmental sector②; (5) reducing or exempt the debt of the poorest nations③; (6) actively assisting developing countries in human resources development, include provide trainings④; (7) opening market for developing countries and exempt custom duties. In addition, China should actively participate in global poverty reduction. IFIs had done a large amount of analysis over poverty reduction in cooperation with the less developed regions in China and formed a clear strategic framework to continue support the Chinese government to develop the less developed areas in China. We should actively participate in the global sustainable development process and focus on environment, natural resources, and water treatment to collaborate with the tenth five-year plan and the sustainable development strategy of developing the west.

① For example, China has established 117 enterprises in Africa, the cooperation in energy, new high technology areas between two sides has been starting; further opening up the markets, China exempts the custom tax for the importing merchandize from least develop countries in Africa.

② For example, actively promoting the cooperation with the African countries on the areas of protection of communicable diseases such as AIDS, Malaria and TB, protection of natural disasters and environment protection; through regional, sub-regional cooperation to reach the objectives of "friendly, safe and mutual richness of neighborhood".

③ For Example, Chinese Government honored in advance its commitment to waive the RMB10.5B debt of 31 African countries to China.

④ For example, China has trained 7,000 persons for African countries, is planning increasing 33% of funds contribution to Africa Human Resources Development Fund to train 10,000 persons in the next 3 years.

8.3 Appendix

8.3.1 Interaction between IFI and the Chinese Government

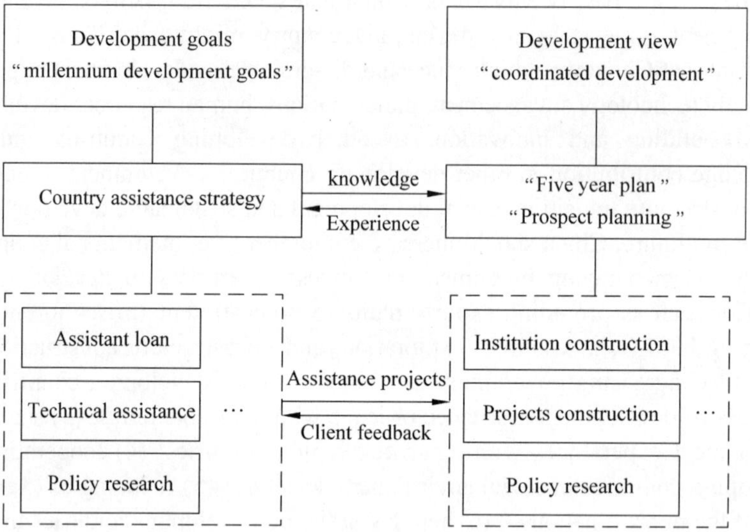

8.3.2 The Change of Weights of FDI and IFI Assistance to GDP

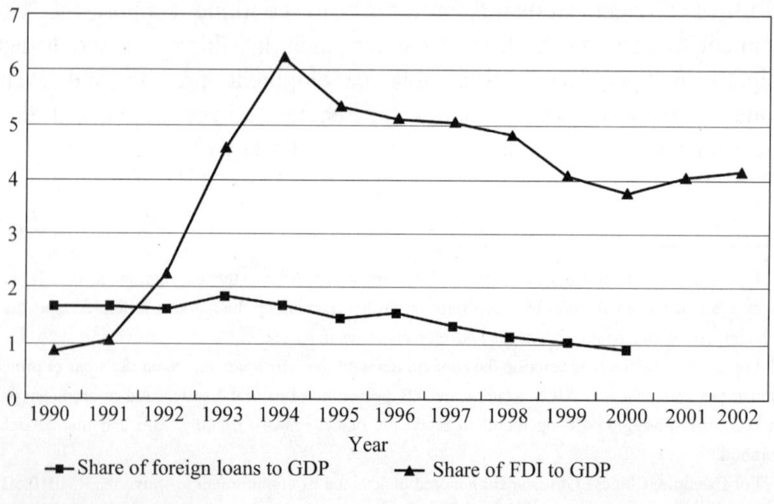

Source: State Statistics Bureau: China Statistic Yearbook (multi years), Beijing: China Statistic Press.

8.3.3 Millennium Development Goals

Goals and targets	Progress Indicators
Goal 1 Eradicate extreme poverty and hunger	
Target 1: Halve, between 1990 and 2015, the proportion of people whose income is less than US$1 a day Target 2: Halve, between 1990 and 2015, the proportion of people who suffer from hunger	• Proportion of population below US$1 a day: 31.3% in 1990, reduced to 10.5% in 1999 • Proportion of population below minimum level of dietary energy consumption: 16.0% in 1990, reduced to 9.0% in 2000
Goal 2 Achieve universal primary education	
Target 3: Ensure that, by 2015, children everywhere, boys and girls alike, will be able to complete a full course of primary schooling	• Net enrollment ratio in primary education: 97.0% in1990, reduced to 93.0% in 2001 • Literacy rate of 15 to 24-year-olds: 95.3% in 1990, increased to 97.9% in 2001
Goal 3 Promote gender equality and empower women	
Target 4: Eliminate gender disparity in primary and secondary education preferably by 2005 and in all levels of education no later than 2015	• Ratio of girls to boys in primary education: 86% in 1990, and 92% in 2001 • Ratio of girls to boys in secondary education: 83% in 2001
Goal 4 Reduce child mortality	
Target 5: Reduce by two-thirds, between 1990 and 2015, the under-five mortality rate	• Under-five mortality rate: 49×10^{-3} in 1990, and reduced to 39×10^{-3} in 2001 • Infant mortality rate: 38×10^{-3} in 1990, and reduced to 31×10^{-3} in 2001
Goal 5 Improve maternal health	
Target 6: Reduce by three-quarters, between 1990 and 2015, the maternal mortality ratio	• Maternal mortality ratio: 0.889×10^{-3} in 1990, and reduced to 0.39×10^{-3} in 2001 • Proportion of births attended by skilled health personnel: 50.6% in 1990, and 89.0% in 2001
Goal 6 Combat HIV/AIDS, malaria, and other diseases	
Target 7: Have halted by 2015 and begun to reverse the spread of HIV/AIDS Target 8: Have halted by 2015 and begun to reverse the incidence of malaria and other major diseases	• By 2001, among HIV/AIDS carriers aged 15 – 49, infection rate 0.11%, approximately 790,000 cases • Malaria incidence rate: 0.01×10^{-3} in 2000 • Tuberculosis incidence rate: 1.07×10^{-3} in 2001
Goal 7 Ensure environmental sustainability	
Target 9: Integrate the principles of sustainable development into country policies and program and reverse the loss of environmental resources	• Proportion of land area covered by forest: 12.98% in 1990, increased to 17% by 2001 • Carbon dioxide emissions (per capita): 2.1 tons in 1990, increased to 2.3 tons in 1999

Continued

Goals and targets	Progress Indicators
Target 10: Halve, by 2015, the proportion of people without sustainable access to safe drinking water and basic sanitation Target 11: Have achieved, by 2020, a significant improvement in the lives of at least 100 million slum dwellers	• Proportion of rural population with sustainable access to safe water source: 60% in 1990, and increased to 66% in 2000 • Proportion of urban population with sustainable access to safe water source: 99% in 1990, reduced to 94% in 2000 • Proportion of urban population with access to clean sanitation: 56% in 1990, increased to 69% in 2000
Goal 8 Develop a global partnership for development	
Target 12: Deal comprehensively with the debt problems of developing countries through national and international measures Target 13: Provide access to affordable, essential drugs in developing countries Target 14: Make available the benefits of new technologies, especially information and communications	• Debt service as a percentage of exports of goods and services: 10.6% in 1990, 4.2% in 2001 • Proportion of population with access to affordable essential drugs on a sustainable basis: 80% – 94 % in 1999 • Telephone lines and cellular subscribers per 100 population: 0.6 in 1990, increased to 24.8 in 2001

Source: July 2003, UNDP, Human Development Report 2003.

a: January 2003, World Bank, Country Assistance Strategy 2003 – 2005.

b: Based on the Human Development Report 2003 of UNDP, July 2003. These data are preliminary and need to be corrected.

8.3.4 The World Bank and Asian Development Bank Strategies to Match the Chinese Government Strategies

Chinese government a	World Bank b	Asian Development Bank c
Rural development: Instead of continuing to focus on food self-sufficiency, the Government will place more emphasis on raising rural incomes. Fiscal reform will reduce the tax burden of farmers. Off-farm employment opportunities will be created. Farmers will be allowed to sell their land-use rights to allow for economies of scale in agriculture and to exit from the sector.	Investment climate: Support for urban and rural development; Infrastructure services to support private sector development Regulatory reform and competition policy; Financial sector reform. Public Sector Governance: Rule of Law (incl. anti-corruption);	Promote equitable and inclusive growth: Increasing infrastructure construction lending in the poor interior regions; Contributing to designing rural finance and rural development reform; Supporting social security system reform;

Continued

Chinese government a	World Bank b	Asian Development Bank c
Urbanization: Accelerating urbanization and coordinating the development of large, medium, and small cities and small towns were identified as ways to address the disappointing performance of the agriculture sector and emerging urban unemployment.	Public administration and civil services reform (incl. public expenditure accountability); Access to and administration of justice (judicial reform).	Promote pro-poor fiscal system reform; And contributing to improving the efficiency of poverty reduction policies and programs.
Private sector promotion: Establishing a level playing field for both domestic and foreign companies and ending policy biases that favor state companies. Legal protection will be provided to income and property, whether derived from labor or from investment.	Empowerment, Security and Social Inclusion: Gender mainstreaming, civic engagement and participation; Social risk management (incl. risk mitigation).	Make markets work better: Improving legal and legislation system, contributing to the development of a transparent regulation framework; Contributing to a favorable environment to promote private sector development; Contributing to remove infrastructure barriers; Supporting financial system reform; Supporting private sector development; And substantially increase ADB lending for private sector operations.
Job creation and social security: Creating more jobs through small and medium enterprise development, particularly in the services sector. The old-age pension, medical insurance, unemployment insurance, and subsistence allowances for urban residents will be improved and some of the restrictions on labor mobility will be removed.	Education: Education for All—with emphasis on girls' education; Building human capacity for the knowledge economy Health: Access to clean water, air and sanitation by poor people;	
Central and western development: Developing the poor interior regions by restructuring the agriculture and industry sectors in the central region and infrastructure and environmental improvement in the western region. Funds will be provided through budget transfers and tax incentives. Economic cooperation will be strengthened between the eastern and interior provinces.	Maternal and child health care. contagious: HIV/AIDS, tuberculosis, malaria and childhood diseases, incl. relevant link to education; Vaccines and drug development for major communicable diseases in developing countries;	Foster regional cooperation: Addressing policy and institutional barriers to regional cooperation; Contributing to remove infrastructure and other barriers to cross-border trade and investment; Supporting private sector investment;

Continued

Chinese government a	World Bank b	Asian Development Bank c
Improving income distribution: Reducing inequalities between rural and urban residents, between regions, and among individuals by enlarging the middle-income class and increasing the incomes of the low-income group. Education: Senior secondary education will be made universal and illiteracy eliminated. The private sector will be encouraged to invest in education. Rule of law: Courts and prosecutors will operate independently and impartially according to law and enforcement of judgments will be improved. Improving transparency and law enforcement will strengthen anticorruption activities. SOE reform: State-owned enterprise (SOE) management systems will be strengthened and some SOEs will be sold, merged, or closed. Monopoly industries, including power, railways, and telecommunications, will be reformed to introduce competition. Markets will be developed for property rights, land, labor, and technology. Government functions will be separated from enterprise management.	Environmental concerns: Climate change, water, forests; Biodiversity, ozone depletion and land degradation Promotion of agricultural research; Trade and integration: Market access; Intellectual property rights and standards. Information and knowledge: Redressing the Digital Divide and equipping countries with the capability to access knowledge; Understanding development and poverty reduction; International financial architecture; Development of international standards; Financial stability (incl. sound public debt management); International accounting and legal framework.	Enforcing regional economic surveillance and regional financial infrastructure; Improve the environment: Contributing to environment related legislation, policies and rules, and institutional reform; Contributing to the use of market-based instruments, clean production technologies, and renewable energy; Combating land degradation and improving management over water pollution, air pollution, and solid waste disposals; And promoting the participation of private sectors and general public in environmental services.

Source: a. Statements made by Zhu Rongji during the 10th National People's Congress in March 2003.

b. World Bank: China Assistance Strategy (2003 – 2005), The World Bank Group, January 2003.

c. Asian Development Bank: China Country Strategy and Program (2004 – 2006), November 2003.

8.3.5 World Bank and Asian Development Bank Assistance Focuses in China

Item	Asian development bank	World bank
Country strategy	Country Strategy and Program (2004 – 2006): Promoting pro-poor inclusive economic growth; Building an enabling environment for the private sector and strengthening public sector governance; Fostering regional cooperation; Promoting environmental sustainability	Country Assistance Strategy (2003 – 2005): Improve the business environment and help accelerate the transition to a market economy; Address the needs of the poorer and disadvantaged people and underdeveloped regions; Facilitate an environmental sustainable development process
Key sectors	Transportation, social infrastructure, agriculture and natural resources, energy, environmental	Transportation, municipal projects (environmental), social sector, energy, water management, agriculture
Key areas	84% of the total lending will be channeled to the projects in central and west part of China during 2004 and 2006	3/4 of the projects will be focused on supporting interior provinces
Assistance scale	Lending: US$1.3 to 1.5 billion per annum (2004 – 2006) Technical Assistance Grant: US$12 to 14 million per annum	US$1.2 to 1.3 billion per annum (2003 – 2005)
Partnership agreement in discussion	PRC-GEF Partnership on Operational Program 12 (OP12) in combating land degradation; Poverty Reduction Cooperation Fund; French Development Agency in Greater Mekong Sub region (GMS) in Yunnan; Provincial Poverty Reduction Agreement with DFID (proposed)	GEF on Renewable Energy; GEF, EU on Sustainable Forestry Project; AusAID on distance learning in Ningxia; Health Project with DFID and CIDA (proposed)

Source: Asian Development Bank, Country Strategy and Program (2004 – 2006), November 2003.

References

[1] International Deptment. MOF: Collection of Documents on IFI Loans Management. Beijing: China Financial and Economic Press, 2001. p.250

[2] Wen Jiabao. Speech at China Africa Cooperation Forum. Xinhua News Agency, December 15,2003

9 Appendix

9.1 World Bank, Asian Development Bank and China

9.1.1 World Bank and China

The World Bank Group is the largest and most influential multilateral aid organization, comprised of five agencies, namely International Bank for Reconstruction and Development (IBRD), the International Development Association (IDA), the International Finance Corporation (IFC), the Multilateral Investment Guarantee Agency (MIGA) and the International Center for the Settlement of Investment Disputes (ICSID). Providing China with sovereign loans are IBRD and IDA.

9.1.1.1 Development Strategy of the World Bank (WB)

Although the World Bank Group is a practical international economic organization, it is not an academic organization. Yet, it has a contingent of high-level researchers in development economics. It has invited noted economists who are influential in the international academic circles to take up the post as chief economist and concurrently as vice-president in charge of research. The posts are set to have a term of three years in order to prevent rigidity and lagging theoretically. Noted economists William H. Chenery, lrving Fisher, Lawrence Summers, Michael Bruno and Joseph E. Stiglitz all held such posts. The orientation of the operations of the group is, to a large extent, directed by the mainstream development economics. Since the 1950's, the operational policy strategy of the World Bank Group has undergone several changes.

1. From the end of the 1950's to the mid – 1960's

Capital formation and accumulation is the key to the economic development of less-developed economies. Economic growth is the source of welfare of the common people and will naturally bring about a higher level of living standards.

Structuralism and investment-led idea based on two-gap model were the guiding principle for the operational policies of the World Bank at the time. During this period, the group mainly supported borrowing countries to develop infrastructure, agricultural and import-substitute industrial projects that required huge investments and were beyond their financial capabilities. In order to help low-income countries with seriously inadequate savings, major developed countries headed by the United States founded IDA to transfer capital to these countries in preferential terms.

2. From the end of the 1960's to the beginning of the 1980's

Poverty became the focus of development economics. The heart of the operation of the World Bank during this period was to satisfy the basic human needs of poor people.

Since the beginning of the 1960's, some developing countries, although achieving economic growth that attracted worldwide attention, the poor population increased instead of being reduced. The benefits brought about by economic growth did not fall naturally to the poor. The World Bank and economists of University of Sussex (UK) advanced the idea of "growth redistribution" in the 1970's. This approach does not exclude growth as the objective, but stresses redistribution of the benefits of growth. According to this approach, economic growth is not enough to increase the welfare of the poor and it is necessary to re-adjust the orientation of investment and redistribute income and consumption in favor of the poor and shift productive assets to the poor. Under the guidance of this theory, nearly all the major development aid organizations adjusted their aid strategies in an attempt to directly alleviate poverty.

3. From 1980's to the beginning of the 1990's

Market-oriented economic structure adjustment and policy reform became the mission of development aid. It is, in essence, to reduce or thoroughly eliminate direct intervention by the state in production and distribution.

Since the beginning of the 1980's, a major turn took place in development economics. Neoclassic Economics, represented by economists of the Chicago School of Economics replaced structuralism to become the mainstream of development economics. Theoretically, it stressed government intervention and the role of market and private sector instead of public sector in economic takeoff.

After summing up and evaluating the experience of the previous 20 years, a large amount of empirical studies enabled economists to renew their understanding of the role of development aid. Many scholars held the opinion that investment-centered aid could not revolve the development problems of recipient countries, because in many developing countries, economic laggardness was caused by their improper policies that resulted in the distortion of the economic environment. Under such environment, it was impossible for outside investment to display its efficiency. So the mission of development aid should be to direct and support developing countries to make market-oriented economic structural adjustments and policy reforms to reduce government intervention and help recipient countries build market mechanisms. The whole of the 1980's was a decade of restructuring.

4. The 1990's

With poverty, environmental protection and institutional building as the theme, the World Bank focused its policies on the following six aspects: poverty reduction, supporting reform and development of the private sector, environmental protection, human resources development, reduction of debt burdens of developing countries and promotion of direct investment.

After entering the 1990's, the World Bank began to show concern about the negative effect of restructuring and reconsidered the role of the government in economic growth. Even Neoclassic economists began to change their attitude, becoming aware of the role of the government not only in management of the market but also in many areas, such as environmental protection, other than the free market. The market and the government should be mutually complementary instead of being mutually exclusive.

During this period, the World Bank had plural focuses. In the 1990's, it focused on investment in social development, with emphasis put on education and public health; in the 21st century, it stresses institutional building, legal construction, environmental protection and participation of poor people. This may be summed up as two models. One is the state creates and improves the investment environment, including both domestic and foreign and both hardware and software; the other is human resource investment, including mastery of advanced means, participation in social and economic development. It redefined poverty.

5. Since the beginning of the 21st century

It has summed up an important experience in the development of the 1990's, that is, the role of public policy in serving the poor is more important than anticipated but it is more difficult to execute than anticipated. The World Bank has thus placed governance and institutions high on its agenda, with more emphasis being put on helping recipient countries to formulate policies for providing effective public services to the poor. During this period, great changes have taken place in the role of the World Bank. It has focused its stress on the learning, mastery and transmission of new knowledge.

9.1.1.2 Evaluation Mechanism and Methodology of the World Bank

Foreign aid, represented by the World Bank, is mostly granted in the form of projects. The aid evaluation of the World Bank is generally divided into two levels: One is done at the micro level, that is, the project level. The main evaluation method is benefit-cost analysis or cost-effectiveness analysis. The evaluation is done project by project, with the success rate as the main indicator. The other is done at the macro level, that is, the impact of loans on economic growth and poverty reduction, that is, to evaluate the general effect of aid, which is divided into sector/thematic analysis and country analysis.

Over the past more than 30 years, the World Bank has developed a set of stringent evaluation system, which is regarded as the most effective evaluation tool and methodology among multilateral development banks.

9.1.1.3 World Bank in China

1. Origin

China began to borrow from the World Bank in 1981, when the country just started reform and opening up and was in urgent need of external financial support to alleviate the shortages in funds and personnel and the backwardness in technology and management. After extensive investigation of the whole economy and priority development sectors, the World Bank identified higher education as an area of high urgency in need of investment.

In June 1981, the World Bank and the Chinese government decided to make university development as the first World Bank loan project. The investment was US$295 million in total, including US$200 million from the World Bank and 145 million yuan domestic. Then an agreement was signed on November 4 of the same year.

Up to August 1986, the university development project was completed on schedule, with civil engineering projects covering a floor space of 323,677 square meters completed, 10,642 sets of advanced equipment purchased, more than 400 foreign experts invited to lecture in China and 2,676 people sent abroad to pursue further study. Twenty-eight project universities built 46 lab centers of the advanced level of the 1980's. The enrolment of undergraduates and postgraduates doubled and redoubled.

2. An overview of World Bank loans to china in past 20 years

With the development of universities as the start, World Bank loans began to increase year by year until it reached US$1.5 billion annually. Up to the mid-1990s, that is, in 1993, 1994 and 1995, the annual loans reached the peak of US$3 billion. Starting from 1996, in view of the realities of successive years of economic growth, the World Bank intentionally reduced the amount of loans to China and the figure returned to an annual US$1.5 billion in 2000. For the annual changes in World Bank loan (see Fig. 9.1).

Among the US$ 34.2 billion total amount of loans committed by the World Bank, US$9.66 billion went to agriculture (accounting for 28.26%), the biggest amount, US$8.13 billion went to communications (23.78%), US$6.33 billion, to energy source development (18.51%), US$2.845 billion, to industry (8.32%), US$2.148 billion, to environmental protection (6.28%), US$1.7 billion, to education (4.96%) and US$3.377 billion, to other sectors (9.88%) (see Fig. 9.2).

In the latter half of the 1990's, the World Bank began to adjust its lending policy toward China. In 1997, it stopped lending to industrial projects; in 1999, it began to reduce loans to thermal-power projects. After providing 10 batches of

Figure 9.1 Amount of World Bank loan's in 1981 – 2000 (in millions of US dollars)

Source: http://www.worldbank.org.cn

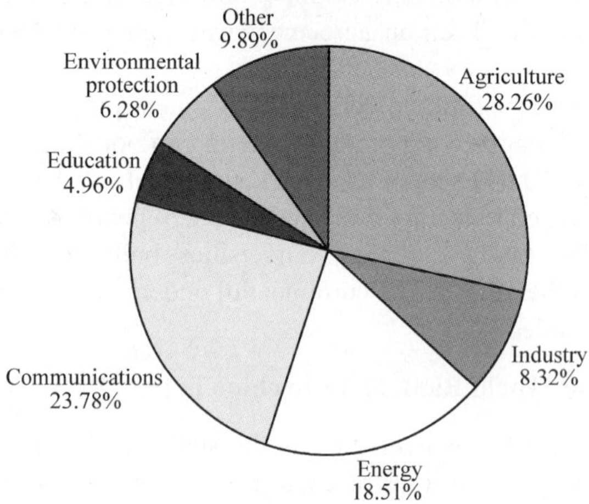

Figure 9.2 World Bank loans to various sectors in 1981 – 2003

Source: http://www.worldbank.org.cn

loans to railway projects, it slowed down. Currently, WB lending is biased toward water supply and wastewater treatment, communications, environmental protection and agriculture.

In terms of regional distribution, coastal areas got the biggest chunk of WB loans, about 46.42% (US$13.3 billion), almost the same as the middle and western parts of the country, US$7.69 billion (middle part) and US$7.66 billion (western part), accounting for 26.84 and 26.74%, respectively. Most of the coastal areas including Shanghai, Zhejiang, Jiangsu and Guangdong and a minority areas in the middle and western parts, including Sichuan, Henan and Hubei got the biggest amount of WB loans and other provinces got less (see Fig. 9.3).

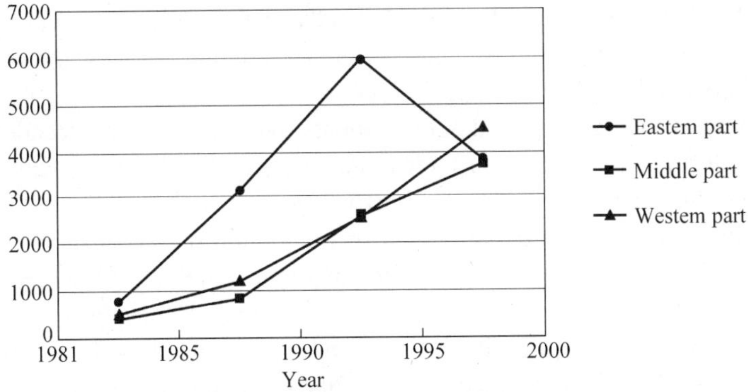

Figure 9.3 World Bank loans to eastern, western and middle parts of China 1981 – 2000

Source: http://www.worldbank.org.cn

3. Major achievements over the past 20 years of cooperation between China and the World Bank

The World Bank is, in fact, an extremely important witness to and a participant in China's reform over the past two decades.

The World Bank loans have been extended almost to all sectors of the national economy and most of the provinces, municipalities and autonomous regions (except Tibet). Loans used by infrastructure projects (communications, energy, industry and city construction) made up more than half. The rest went to agriculture, social sectors (education, health and social security), environmental protection, water supply and environmental sanitation. All these projects have played a direct or indirect role in reducing poverty.

The more than 20 years of reform and opening up have brought about earthshaking changes to China's economy. The achievements that are attractive worldwide are the two-digit growth and the shaking off of absolute poverty for hundreds of millions of people. In fact, China's contribution to the reduction of poverty in the world over the past two decades is bigger than any other country in the world. According to the World Bank estimates, the total population in poverty in 1987 – 1998 was reduced by 8 million while the poor population in areas other than China in the world increased by 82 million. The rapid economic growth and effective poverty-relief policy have enabled China to realize its international development objective ahead of time, that is, to reduce poverty to half of the 1990's level before 2015.

Apart from increasing income, the market-oriented reform over the past 20 years has not only injected renewed vigor into urban and rural economy but also helped improve the human development indicators. Official estimates show that the adult literacy rate has been reduced by more than half, from 37% in 1978 to 17% by 1999, while the mortality rate of infants was reduced from 4.1% to 3%.

While the economy has developed rapidly, the urbanization level has risen. Twenty years ago, 70% of the population were agricultural, but now the percentage has been reduced to 50%.

In view of the development achievements over the past two decades, China graduated from IDA (which provides the poorest developing countries with interest-free loans) and it is now only borrowing from IBRD.

Not only so, with the development of the capital market, China's financial situation has improved, the interest rates at home have been lowered and the financing channels have been diversified. Its demand for outside funds has become less and less, especially in the economically developed countries. This indicates that China has changed from a fund-short and capital market lagged country to one with relatively adequate capital.

In this process, although we can not say for sure how much contribution the World Bank has made, it is no doubt that the World Bank is one of the very active factors.

4. China's contribution to the World Bank

China is not only the biggest borrower from the World Bank but also one of the countries that have World Bank projects best performed. The cooperation between China and the World Bank has not only promoted China's development but also stimulated the development of the World Bank. China has used most of the loans from the World Bank to improve the ecological system, poverty reduction and other areas for sustainable development. The quality of World Bank projects performed by China is so high that it can be held up as a "good example in cooperation with the World Bank" (Jin Liqun, 2003), which has, to a great extent, enriched the experience of the World Bank in providing loans and improving the quality of its capital operation, making it more attractive.

During the cooperation with the World Bank, China listens to the suggestions from the World Bank but does not follow them without any judgment. It draws on both the experience of the World Bank and considers the actual national conditions of China. The relationship between China and the World Bank is a new and equal one as between an international organization and a member of developing countries.

The whole of the 1980's and the upper middle of the 1990's, the World Bank provided loans to China mainly for construction projects, when capital was no longer the principal bottleneck, the demand for knowledge, technology and diversified services increased, thus providing further incentives for this aid agency to transit to knowledge-intensive operations. After the latter half of the 1990's, World Bank loans began to be used in a diversity of projects, with more stress being put on knowledge transfer and analysis and policy counseling on more difficult problems.

9.1.2 Asian Development Bank and China

1. Origin

When the ADB was founded, Taiwan was a member in the name of "China". On February 17, 1986, the ADB Council adopted a resolution to accept the People's Republic of China. On March 10, the same year, China became a full ADB member, but Taiwan continued to remain in it in the name of "Chinese Taipei".

In December 1986, ADB approved the first US$75,000 technical aid to the Changshan Power Plant under the China Huaneng Power Company for shifting its fuel from oil to coal. This was the first deal between ADB and China. After that, the relations of friendship and cooperation between China and ADB have continued to develop. By the end of 2000, China became the second largest borrower and the largest recipient of technical aid and donations of ADB, receiving US$10.181 billion hard loans for 80 projects and nearly US$200 million technical aid for 370 projects and donations from ADB.

The main part of the ADB loans was used in infrastructure and agricultural projects with the guarantee by the Chinese Ministry of Finance, with about 60% for infrastructure facilities. The ADB loans were mostly directed at the eastern part of the country in the early period. It gradually moved to the western part starting from the middle and late period of the 1990's.

2. An overview of ADB's China projects in the last 14 years

As shown in Fig. 9.4, the total ADB loans in 1987, 1988 and 1989 were small and fluctuated owing to political reasons. Starting from 1990, ADB loans had risen successively until 1995 when it reached US$1.2 billion and it began to drop slightly in 1996 and 1997. In the three years after that, there were rises and falls.

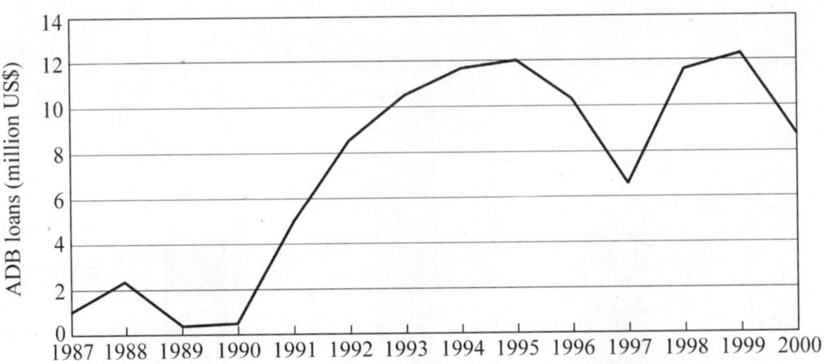

Figure 9.4 Annual distribution of ADB loans to China

Source: ADB China Office

As compared with the World Bank, ADB shows clearer bias toward priority sectors such communications and transport, which is overwhelmingly the emphasis of ADB investment. The total investment in this sector has reached US$5 billion, 48.8% of the total loans to China. It is followed by the energy sector, with US$1.776 billion (17.45%), agriculture, with US$844 million (8.29%), social and public service, with US$820 million (8.05%), industry with US$687 million (6.75%), environment, with US$556 million (5.45%) and finance, with US$530 million (5.21%), just as shown in Fig. 9.5.

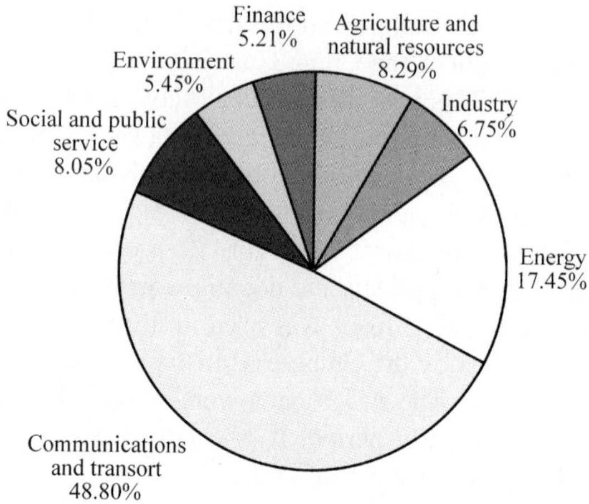

Figure 9.5 Sectoral distribution of ADB loans to China

Source: ADB China Office

Apart from the differences in total amount and sectional emphasis, ADB and the World Bank are identical in regional distribution of their loans. Just as shown in Fig. 9.6, both ADB and the World Bank use nearly 50% of the total loan to China in the eastern part of the country, with ADB more biased towards the

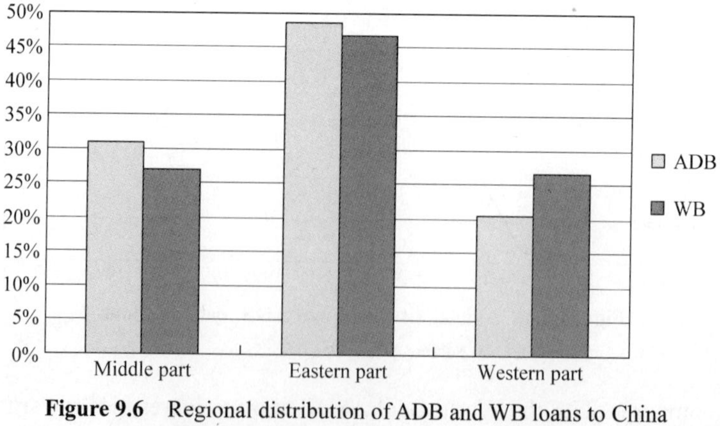

Figure 9.6 Regional distribution of ADB and WB loans to China

Source: ADB China Office, WB China Office

eastern and middle parts than the World Bank. The total ADB loans in the eastern and middle parts of China made up 79.5% while WB loans in the two parts of the country accounted for 70.5%.

3. Achievements in the close cooperation between China and ADB

ADB loans to China have played a positive and useful role in easing fund shortages, in importing advanced technology and management experience, in removing bottlenecks in communications and energy sources and in stimulating economic growth, reducing poverty and protecting the environment.

ADB has made contributions to reducing poverty and improving the living standards of the Chinese people by promoting sustainable and poverty-relief economic development and supporting unemployment and development in the poor middle and western parts of the country. It has also stimulated the development of management systems required by the market economy, strengthened environmental protection and natural resources management and cultivated the non-governmental sector of the economy and encouraged regional cooperation.

By using ADB loans, China has constructed 3,000 kilometers of free ways, 5,515 kilometers of railways and improved 4,500 kilometers of highways that connected poor counties.

4. China's contribution to ADB

The successful cooperation between China and ADB has not only given a powerful support to China's development, but also enriched the development theories and operational practice of ADB itself. Most of the ADB loan projects are good in cycle, quality, budget implementation and repayment of loans, setting a successful example for reducing poverty and promoting development in the Asian region.

9.2 Study and Evaluation Methodology

9.2.1 Post-Project Evaluation

Post-project evaluation is an indispensable link in the project life cycle. It uses the actual achievements and efficiency to analyze and evaluate the policy decisions, management and performance of a project and, by drawing on experiences and lessons, serve policy makers and investors and provide reliable basis for new projects. At the same time, such evaluation may provide feedback information to the performance of projects so as to timely adjust construction schemes. It can also carry out diagnosis of short-title projects to provide recommendations and schemes. On the basis of post-project evaluation, policy decision-making departments may analyze and study national, regional or industrial programs and provide the basis for adjusting policies and modifying plans.

The commonly accepted definition of post-project evaluation is: to carry out systematic and objective analysis of the purposes, process of performance, efficiency, functions and impact of a project completed and, through the checking and summary of project activities, establish whether the anticipated goal of the project has been achieved and whether the project is reasonable and effective, whether the major efficiency indicators are realized and through analysis and evaluation, find out reasons for failure and sum up experience and lessons; and through timely and effective information feedback, put forward recommendations for future project decisions and for improving the level of investment policy decision making and management, and at the same time, put forward recommendations for improvement on problems that crop up in the operation of the project evaluated so as to achieve the goal of improving investment efficiency[1].

The definition and characteristics of post-project evaluation show that post-project evaluation plays an important role in raising the scientific level of project policy decision making, improving project management level, overseeing normal production and operation of the project, lowering risks of investment project and raising the efficiency of investment.

When viewed from the world as a whole, it already has a history of nearly 60 years since the first post-project evaluation was done by the US government in the 1930's. But it did not receive full attention from many countries and such bilateral and multilateral aid agencies as the World Bank and the Asian Development Bank until the middle period of the 1970's, when the World Bank and ADB began to apply it extensively in its investment activities in the world.

At present post-project evaluation organizations of all countries vary and are changing with the social and economic development. Before the 1960's, international project evaluation and emphasis of such evaluation were concentrated on financial analysis, which was used as the major indicator for the success or failure of the project evaluated. Up to the 1960's, western countries invested a large amount of funds in energy, communications and telecom and other infrastructure facilities and social welfare from the angle of their own long-term development. The direct financial efficiency of these projects was far from industrial projects. The same was true with the investment by the World Bank and other international financial organizations in less-developed countries. That is why the concept of economic evaluation (national economic evaluation at home) was introduced to the area of project efficiency evaluation.

At around the 1970's, the world economic development brought about serious pollution that caused worldwide concerns. All developed countries and then nearly all other countries promulgated environmental protection laws. According to the requirements of the laws, project evaluation included the environmental impact as part of the contents. After that, with the development of the economy, the project social functions and impact began to arouse the attention of investors, that is, who were the real beneficiaries of investment projects. Up to the 1980's, the World Bank and other organizations showed great concern for the impact of their aid projects on the poor people, especially women, social culture and sustainable development. Therefore, social impact evaluation became one of the important contents of the evaluation of investment activities. Besides, foreign aid organizations have in recent years become aware that organizational setup and management mechanism are the important conditions for the success of a project, thus the analysis of organizational setup has also become part and parcel of project evaluation.

In general, the development process of post-project evaluation assumes the following three characteristics:

(1) Contents and methodologies of evaluation have developed towards diversification, experiencing single financial evaluation to multiple evaluation covering financial affairs and the impact on the economy, environment and social affairs and the contents and targets of evaluation have increased;

(2) Project evaluation tends to cover the whole process of investment project;

(3) International financial organizations have expanded the functions of post-project evaluation organizations and, together with budget, monitoring, auditing and evaluation, formed an effective and complete management cycle and evaluation system.

The post-investment project evaluation in China started in the middle of the 1980's and it spread nationwide up to the middle of the 1990's and initially formed its own post-project evaluation system. With the deepening and development of the investment system reform, the pre-project evaluation and project decision-making have been strengthened and post-project evaluation has gradually won the full attention of the economic and investment circles. Apart from that of key state construction projects and projects financed by international financial institutions and state banks, post-project evaluation has also proceeded well in such projects in agriculture, forestry, energy development, communications and public health. In general, the post-project evaluation and study and practical work are still in the initial stage and it still lacks systematic study and its application has not become widespread.

9.2.2 Common Methodologies in Post-Project Evaluation

Till today, post-project evaluation development is largely divided into three periods: 1830 – 1930, which was a starting period, with French engineer Jules Dupuit (1804 – 1866) applied the concept of diminishing marginal utility and cost-effectiveness of public works; 1930 – 1968, which was a period of development and application of the traditional cost-effectiveness analysis method. Before 1960, the method was applied in the water conservancy and public works of the United

States and achieved initial development. After 1960, the method went deeper and improved and its application was extended from public works to industry, agriculture and other economic sectors and spread from the United States to Europe and developing countries. Project evaluation thus became a systematic theoretical and methodological system and post-project evaluation method improved markedly. From 1968 to present is a period of emergence and application of new methods, when OECD and UNIDO advanced the modern cost-effectiveness analysis (Huang Dechun and Xu Changxin, 2003) and the post-project evaluation analysis also developed from the traditional economic analysis to quantitative and qualitative analysis, with qualitative analysis as the main body. The most commonly used methods are:

9.2.2.1 Comparison

One of the main contents of post-project evaluation is to re-evaluate the conclusions of the pre-project evaluation and, through comparison between the actual project data and the anticipated data, make analysis and evaluation of the performance and management of projects. The comparison principle has thus become a main principle for post-project evaluation, including before and after comparison, actual data and predicted data comparison and with and without comparison.

Before and after comparison refers to a method of comparing the situations before the project is performed and after it is completed to determine the efficiency of the project. The post-project evaluation, through the comparison of the preliminary feasibility study and the predicted conclusions and the actual results of the project operation, discovers the changes and analyzes the reasons to determine the quality of plan, policy decision and project performance.

With and without comparison refers to comparison between what really happens when the project is performed and what might happen when the project is not performed in order to measure the real efficiency, impact and functions of a project. In making with and without comparisons, it is, first of all, necessary to carry out investigations into the social conditions of the project areas when the project is not proposed and the social conditions of the project areas after the project is completed. Such comparative analysis determines what social changes the project has brought about, that is, the nature and degree of all kinds of benefits and impact. The emphasis of comparison is to distinguish between the impact of project roles and the impact of extra-project roles. Such comparison is mainly applied in evaluating project efficiency and impact.

9.2.2.2 Interest Group Analysis

Interest group refers to all parties that have direct or indirect immediate interests in projects and that have direct or indirect impact on the success of the project, such as project beneficiaries, project victims and governmental and non-governmental organizations associated with the project. The interest group analytical method must, first of all, make a short list of project interest groups and then evaluate their roles in and their importance to the success of the project and in the end decide on what measures should be taken concerning the interest groups in the process of project performance.

9.2.2.3 Logical Framework Analysis (LFA)

This is a practically effective method adopted by many countries at present. Usually it starts by developing a Problem Tree, trying to identify what is the real problem the project is to tackle, then consider the direct causes of the problem and next, repeat the process and continue to repeat as necessary. All the statements must be written in negative terms. This will give a problem tree in which a cause and effect relationship operates from the bottom to the top. It may also work upwards from the original problem, identifying its effect. Then changing the wording of each item into positive terms will change the Problem Tree into an Objective Tree. Next, decide whether the original problem is still going to be the main focus (or goal) of the project. After making that decision, the purpose, output and activities should be present in the Objective Tree (See Fig. 9.7).

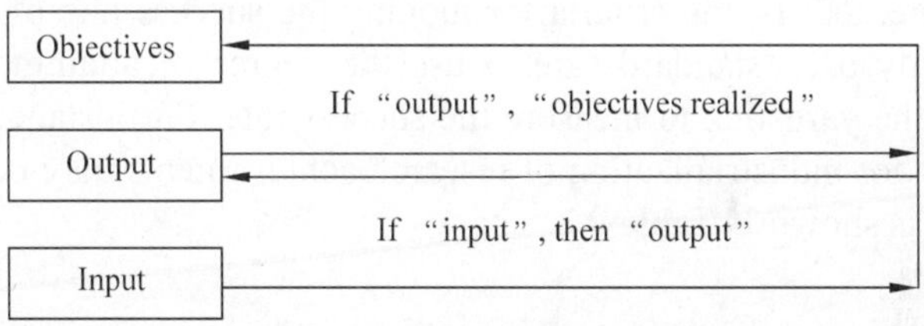

Figure 9.7 Vertical logic diagram of the logical framework analysis

Further work will be done by horizontal analysis, with the logical relations making up of original goal, actual results, cause analysis and sustainable conditions. Together with the vertical logical relations, it forms a logical framework of post-project evaluation (see Table 9.1).

Table 9.1 Horizontal logic of LFA

	Original objectives	Actual results	Cause analysis	Sustainable conditions
Input				
Process of performance				
Results of performance				
Impact				
Project objectives				

The purpose of post-project evaluation of LFA is to establish the logical relationship at different levels of objectives according to the materials and then use LDA to analyze the project efficiency, effectiveness, impact and sustainability so as to facilitate the finding of the causal relationship among different factors and lead to more systematic and comprehensive thinking of problems and prevent major loopholes. At the same time, LFA is to seek causes from results, thus facilitating the identification of the causes for project failure and summing up of experience and lessons.

9.2.2.4 Project Overall Evaluation—Success Rate Evaluation Method

Success rate evaluation method is commonly used in comprehensive project evaluation. It uses the conclusions about the realization of project objectives, economic efficiency analysis and sustainability evaluation from LFA and relies on the experience of evaluators and evaluating group in making qualitative conclusions of the success rate of project.

1. Standards for project success rate

In evaluating project success rate, it is, therefore, necessary to formulate standards for success rate, that is, the criteria for judging the success rate of projects. The most commonly used standards are to use the degree of attainment of project objectives as the yardstick to measure the success rate. For instance, the success rate of project for industrialization of research achievements may be divided into four scales as is shown in Table 9.2.

Table 9.2 Division of success grades of project

	Objectives	Efficiency
Highly successful, AAA	all are fulfilled or over-fulfilled	Good, with big impact
Successful, AA	Most objectives realized	Anticipated efficiency and impact achieved
Partly successful, A	Part of the objectives realized	Having certain efficiency and impact
Unsuccessful, B	Objectives not achieved	No efficiency or impact

2. Steps and methods for measuring success rate

(1) Make success rate evaluation sheet, which should include major indicators of projects under evaluation;

(2) Establish the correlation of the indicators in the sheet with project according to the type and characteristics of specific projects and divide them into "important" and "non-important" and fill them in the second column. The "non-important" indicators need not to be measured;

(3) Evaluate the success rate of each indicator, divided into four scales: AAA, AA, A and B. Put the conclusions and importance of indicators together and arrive at success rate evaluation conclusion of the whole project.

3. Success rate evaluation sheet

The making of success rate evaluation sheet should vary according to the objectives and nature of different projects. The post-project evaluation for project of industrialization of research achievements may use the Table 9.3.

Table 9.3 Project success rate evaluation sheet

Evaluation indicators of project execution	Correlative importance	Success rate
Objective: Degree of realization		
Degree of advance nature of technology Product reliability Efficiency: profitability on investment profitability on sales annual interest rates input/output ratio		
Market: product demand competitiveness market share		
Impact: environment institutional building		
Sustainability: funds personnel marketing requirements policy macro environment (domestic and international)		
Total success rate		

9.2.3 Contents of Post-Project Evaluation

Post-project evaluation covers a very complicated technical economics analysis work, covering a wide area. A set of scientific and effective indicator system is of great importance in evaluating the success rate of a project. In configuring and selecting indicators, it is necessary to follow the principle of integrating comprehensiveness, purpose, comparability, dynamic indicators and static indicators, integrating comprehensive indicators with single indicators and integrating micro-investment result indicators with macro-investment result indicators. The existing literature show that post-project evaluation does not have a set of commonly accepted indicator system. We shall relate them according to the components of the evaluation system.

Based on the development of modern post-project evaluation theory, post-project evaluation should include completion and acceptance, post-evaluation of project efficiency and post-evaluation of project management. This study concerns mainly the latter two.

9.2.3.1 Project Completion and Acceptance

Project completion and acceptance is a hallmark of production, use and operation of investment project. At this stage, major achievements are report on project completion, which is also the basis for the next two stages. As this is not the main content of this study, we shall not go into it.

9.2.3.2 Post-Evaluation of Project Efficiency

Post-evaluation of project efficiency is an important component part of the post-project evaluation theory. Based on the efficiency (economic, environment and social) and its hidden technical impact, it re-calculates the economic data to obtain related investment result indicators and then compares them with related economic results values (such as NPV, IRR and investment recoup period) predicted by the pre-project evaluation, social and environment impact (such as IEQ), evaluates and analyzes deviations and causes and draws on experience and lessons so as to serve the purpose of improving the investment management level and investment policy decision making. A complete project efficiency evaluation system should include objective evaluation, process evaluation, cost-benefit evaluation, impact evaluation and sustainability evaluation.

1. Objective evaluation

Major measuring items of objective evaluation should include whether the project is performed according to schedule and whether the project management and monitoring system can ensure real-time feedback of problems in the course of performance and operation. Specifically, objective evaluation is to evaluate the degree of realization of the objectives originally set and is one of the main tasks of post-project evaluation. The post-project evaluation should see the objectives actually realized by using the major indicators originally set, analyze the causes of changes that have occurred so as to judge the degree of realization. The indicators for project objectives should be established before the project proposal. They usually include:

(1) Macro-development objectives, namely, the general impact and roles of the project in the project area or industry or the national economy and social development. These indicators are hard to be quantified. They can only analyzed qualitatively.

(2) Physical objectives, namely, the quantity of products or services provided by the project. These indicators can be analyzed quantitatively.

Another task of objective evaluation is to evaluate the correctness, rationale and practicality of the original policy objectives. Some projects do not have clear objectives or the objectives set do not accord with actual conditions or have changed with the changes of policy or market in the process of performance and all these should be re-analyzed and evaluated in the process of post-project evaluation.

The objective evaluation mainly use before and after and with and without comparisons.

2. Process evaluation

The process evaluation mainly concerns how a project is implemented, with emphasis on checking and identifying problems in the services system by checking all the processes of project proposal decision, designing, procurement and construction against the actual progress and schedule and objectives to find out the causes for the results and identify the links and causes that are successful or unsuccessful, find out the differences between subjective desire and objective reality so as to make future performance of project plans and objectives more conformable to reality.

Process evaluation mainly checks up on the efficiency of project management mechanism, analyzes and evaluates the behavior and participation of participants in the project. It mainly covers the following aspects:

(1) Efficiency of management mechanism: analyze and evaluate the management capability and manager's management skills of project implementation organizations, including contract management, personnel management and training and cooperation with beneficiaries and technical aid, and the use of advisory experts and project monitoring system. It main checks the progress of project and implementation, supporting facilities and services, project management and mechanism, and the implementation of accounting rules;

(2) Behavior of project unit: For investors, it includes project proposal, preparations and evaluation and the decision on the contents and size of projects; for lenders, it is necessary to analyze and evaluate the investment environment and conditions of borrowers, including capabilities of performing agreement, qualifications and credit rating, exercise regulation and control of project and provide conveniences for the operation of project and the scope of beneficiaries and their reactions.

The following quantitative indicators may be used for judging the efficiency of management mechanism in the process evaluation: actual decision taking cycle, changes in the project decision cycle, changes in the design cycle, actual construction period, fixed quota construction period of defense projects, unit average fixed quota construction period, actual construction cost, actual construction cost changes, actual project standard rate, actual number of excellent projects, actual losses caused by re-doing, actual unit production capacity investment, actual investment and changes in actual investment. The analysis mainly uses some quantitative indicators before and after project comparison and without comparison.

3. Cost-benefit evaluation

Cost-benefit evaluation is mainly to analyze project cost, including currency cost and non-currency cost by comparing the actual results generated by projects and the outcome of projects with planned cost and input and profitability in order to judge whether the initial decision of investment pays off. In the process of evaluation, it is necessary to give emphasis to analysis of the opportunity cost and benefits of project.

Cost-benefit evaluation mainly covers cost-effective financial evaluation and national economy evaluation:

(1) Cost-effective financial evaluation. The focal points include profit-taking abilities and project liquidation ability and main indicators include internal gains, net current value, cost-benefit ratio and period of loan repayment and some other debt repayment ability indicators.

(2) National economy evaluation is to examine the expenses and efficiency of projects from the angle of the national economy as a whole and adopt shadow prices, shadow wages, shadow exchange rates and social discount rate and other parameters during different periods, adjust the financial expenses, financial efficiency that actually occur in the years preceding the post-evaluation and the financial expenses and efficiency predicted for various years at the end of the period of calculation after the post-project evaluation and calculate and analyze the net efficiency brought to the national economy and test the actual result of the allocation of social resources.

(3) Impact analysis

Impact evaluation is mainly to analyze if the project operation has produced the anticipated results for individuals, residents and organizations and other results brought about by the project, including both positive and passive. They include the following three aspects: economic impact evaluation: to analyze the impact of projects on the economy at the regional, related industry and the state levels, including employment, domestic resources cost (or exchange cost) and technical progress; environmental impact evaluation: this includes pollution control, regional environmental quality, utilization and protection of natural resources, regional ecological equilibrium and environment management; social impact evaluation: to analyze the tangible and intangible impact on social development, usually including poverty, equality, participation, women and sustainable development.

4. Sustainability impact

Project sustainability refers to whether the established objectives of project can continue after investment and construction are completed and whether the project may develop sustainably, whether the project owner is willing and relies on its own efforts to continue to realize the established objectives, whether the project can be repeated, that is, whether the same projects can be built in the same methods.

Factors influencing sustainability are very complicated, usually including policy, management organization, local participation, financial affairs, technology, culture and ecology. The basic method for sustainability evaluation is based on the summary of the implementation of a given project and a prediction for the future of project. Conventional analytical method is to build a logical framework and use it to analyze conditions and risks associated with projects from the long-term goal, efficiency, outcome, performance and input.

5. Integrated evaluation

Integrated evaluation of project includes the analysis of success or failure of project and responsibilities in various links in project management. It usually adopts the success rate evaluation method, which relies on the experience of evaluation experts or expert group to evaluate the results of all indicators and arrive at quantitative conclusions about the success rate of project. That is commonly known as "expert scoring method".

9.2.3.3 Post-Evaluation of Project Management

Post-evaluation of project management is based on the post evaluation of project completion and acceptance and project efficiency and taking into account management in different stages of the project cycle. The purpose of the evaluation is to know the current project management level through the analysis and study of the management work during different stages and actual conditions to get a general view of the project management and through analysis, comparison and evaluation draw on experience and lessons and ensure better performance of project management in the future and promote a better attainment of the anticipated objectives. Post-evaluation of project management includes process post-evaluation, comprehensive management post-evaluation and evaluation of project managers, taking into account many other external factors influencing the outcome of projects, such as prices, market conditions, natural disasters and political situation as well as associated organizational factors, such as joint financiers, contractors and suppliers.

9.2.4 Post-Evaluation Framework of Some Projects

9.2.4.1 Post-Evaluation Framework of the World Bank Loan Projects

1. Evaluation organization

The post-evaluation organization of the World Bank was founded in 1970. In 1975, the World Bank set up a general superintendent responsible for post-evaluation and officially set up an Operations Evaluation Department (OED). After that, post-evaluation has been brought onto the orbit of important regular management and performance of the World Bank. The main purpose of carrying out post-evaluation is to evaluate objectively the policies, programs, projects and procedures implemented by the World Bank and improve these policies, programs and projects by drawing on experience and lessons.

In order to improve the quality of its loan operations, the World Bank set up a project quality oversight organization—Quality Assurance Group (QAG) in 1998, to be responsible for monitoring and controlling operations quality, check the loan project quality and consulting services and check the quality of projects so as to improve management. The QAG's work is a supplement to the operations vice-president in quality assurance. This reform has helped improve greatly the quality of loan projects. The bad loan proportion dropped from 1/3 to 10%[2].

2. Evaluation standards and contents

In carrying out evaluation, OED follows three standards:

(1) relevance: that is, the relations between aid objectives and the policy and development objectives of recipient countries and between the priority strategy of recipient organizations and the regional and industrial development objectives;

(2) efficacy: that is, the degree of realization of development objectives;

(3) efficiency: the cost-effectiveness in project operations.

Relevance is the most important among the three standards, because only when objectives of development aid are matched with the development strategy and development plan of a country, is it possible to bring about the biggest welfare improvement to recipient countries and regions. In the post-evaluation process, the following indicators should be taken into consideration.

(1) Sustainability: the ability of projects to cope with risks.

Contents of evaluation: what is the mechanism of project to cope with risks? How sensitive is the project to operational environment? Will profitability of the whole project sustain? How does project cope with changes in environment? How about its repair mechanism?

Indicators of evaluation: there are mainly technical, financial and economic indicators, including technology, accounting, economy, social support (including constraints on protective measures), environment, government factor (including both central and local governments and existence of acquisition and merger funds), factors of other stakeholders (including local stakeholders, people of related interests, civil society, non-governmental organizations and private sectors), institutional support (including legal framework, organization and management efficiency), capabilities of coping with external impact (including trade requirements, economic impact, geopolitics and security).

(2) Institutional development impact: the impact of projects on a state or a region in being better able to utilize human capital, capital and natural resources.

Contents of evaluation: (1) implications of institutional arrangements, stability, transparency, enforceability and predictability; (2) comprehensibility and abilities of accomplishment of project units and management level.

Evaluation indicators: institutional development objectives should include: improvement of the environment (law, rules, incentives, competitiveness, culture and customs and conventions) and institutional changes (adding or disappearing, reform or amelioration, technical innovation, supplement, information system, planning or policy analysis).

(3) Outcome: accomplishment of objectives set.

Evaluation contents and indicators: Whether is a project worth started or implemented? What the biggest institutional development and changes will a project bring about? What are the costs and benefits to be generated by projects? What is the economic benefit rate of investment?

(4) Bank performance: degree of participation of the World Bank in the process, including providing services and policy support.

Evaluation contents and indicators: ① quality of access (QoE): the concept, objectives and methods indicated in project proposal. It can be classified into such aspects as technical, economic, environmental, poverty reduction and social, institutional analysis, financial management, project performance and risk management and sustainability; ② regulation: regulation on development impact and evaluation of regulation input and process evaluation.

(5) Borrower's performance: the efforts made by borrowers in designing, preparations and quality of performance, the performance of contracts or agreements and the efforts made toward sustainability of projects.

Evaluation contents: the evaluation is divided into several stages: preparation, performance, cooperation and summation.

In the process of the World Bank operations, post-project evaluation mainly concerns about outcome and results on the basis of various project summary reports. This part of the work is done by OED. The evaluation and control system requires result-based objectives and comprehensiveness and also requires certain timeliness so as to control possible risks cropping up in the operation of projects. In this sense, post-evaluation is a bond connecting with policy formulation, organization learning and knowledge management. It is also the chief means for developing countries to share experiences and carry out exchanges.

3. Characteristics of World Bank post-evaluation framework

The post-evaluation framework of World Bank projects shows that the World Bank mainly carries out post-evaluation of problems that have cropped out from projects on the basis of the project summary reports and the purpose of evaluation includes relevance, effectiveness and efficiency. Such post evaluation is favorable for timely adjustment of projects that have deviated from the aid strategy or development strategy so as to bring the projects back onto the theme of poverty reduction and development. It is also favorable for evaluation organizations to get a good command of the economic conditions of projects and project control costs. Lastly, owing to selectiveness of projects for post-evaluation, it may avoid the same mistakes and lessons in the operation of future projects.

9.2.4.2 Post Evaluation Framework of Projects of International Finance Corporations

International Finance Corporation (IFC) is a member of the World Bank Group. Its purpose is to stimulate economic development by encouraging productive private enterprises and private sector. By investing in the private sector of developing countries, it would stimulate and help its sustainable growth, thus reducing poverty and improving the living standards of the people. Operations Evaluation Group (OEG) is an independent post-evaluation organization of the International Finance Corporation. Like OED, it is directly accountable to Director General of Operation Evaluation. As the IFC mainly lends money to the private sector and does not require government guarantee, the quality of loan projects is the first choice in the post evaluation. Its purpose shows that it uses loan projects as a means for stimulating growth of the private sector and ultimately the development of countries and regions, it determines that the post-project evaluation must cover the two major areas of economic efficiency and development impact.

1. Post-Evaluation framework of IFC

IFC started evaluation in 1996. It has developed its own set of evaluation system after eight years, which has become one of the most effective evaluation methods for multilateral development financial organizations. The evaluation method covers development results, IFC investment impact and IFC work quality. The contents and indicators are shown in Table 9.4.

Table 9.4 Contents and indicators of IFC's post evaluation

	Contents	Indicators
Development Outcome	General impact of comprehensive evaluated project on a country's development	1. Impact on economic development 2. Impact on economic sustainability 3. Impact on environment and society 4. Contribution to private sector development
IFC's Investment Outcome	Impact of project on IFC's financial sustainability and future development	1. General impact of project on IFC loans 2. General impact of project on IFC proprietary rights

Continued

	Contents	Indicators
IFC's Work Quality	Comprehensive evaluation of the quality of IFC's work	1. Identification, evaluation and project proposal 2. Monitoring and Management project execution 3. Involvement in projects

Source: Nicholas Burke, Speech at International Forum on the Evaluation of the Performance of Loans by International Financial Organizations, April, 2004.

After evaluating all aspects of project according to the framework, and make the comprehensive evaluation by using the following table to make projects comparable (Table 9.5).

Table 9.5 Comprehensive evaluation table for the post evaluation of projects financed by IFC

<table>
<tr><td></td><td>Highly unsuccessful</td><td colspan="2">Unsuccessful</td><td>Moderately unsuccessful</td><td>Moderately successful</td><td colspan="2">Successful</td><td>Highly successful</td></tr>
<tr><td>Development results</td><td></td><td colspan="2"></td><td></td><td></td><td colspan="2"></td><td></td></tr>
<tr><td>Project impact</td><td colspan="2">Unsatisfactory</td><td colspan="2">Partly satisfactory</td><td colspan="2">Satisfactory</td><td colspan="2">Very good</td></tr>
<tr><td>Economic development</td><td colspan="2"></td><td colspan="2"></td><td colspan="2"></td><td colspan="2"></td></tr>
<tr><td>Economic sustainability</td><td colspan="2"></td><td colspan="2"></td><td colspan="2"></td><td colspan="2"></td></tr>
<tr><td>Environment and social</td><td colspan="2"></td><td colspan="2"></td><td colspan="2"></td><td colspan="2"></td></tr>
<tr><td>Private sector development</td><td colspan="2"></td><td colspan="2"></td><td colspan="2"></td><td colspan="2"></td></tr>
<tr><td>IFC investment impact</td><td colspan="2"></td><td colspan="2"></td><td colspan="2"></td><td colspan="2"></td></tr>
<tr><td>On IFC loans</td><td colspan="2"></td><td colspan="2"></td><td colspan="2"></td><td colspan="2"></td></tr>
<tr><td>On IFC Proprietary rights</td><td colspan="2"></td><td colspan="2"></td><td colspan="2"></td><td colspan="2"></td></tr>
<tr><td>IFC work quality</td><td colspan="2"></td><td colspan="2"></td><td colspan="2"></td><td colspan="2"></td></tr>
<tr><td>Identification, evaluation and organization of project proposal</td><td colspan="2"></td><td colspan="2"></td><td colspan="2"></td><td colspan="2"></td></tr>
</table>

Continued

	Unsatisfactory	Partly satisfactory	Satisfactory	Very good
Project execution oversight and management				
Participation in project execution				

Source: the same as Table 9.4.

In the process of IFC post evaluation, in order to better learn knowledge and sum up experience from the evaluation, OEG has developed an Evaluation Learning Cycle, as shown in Fig. 9.8.

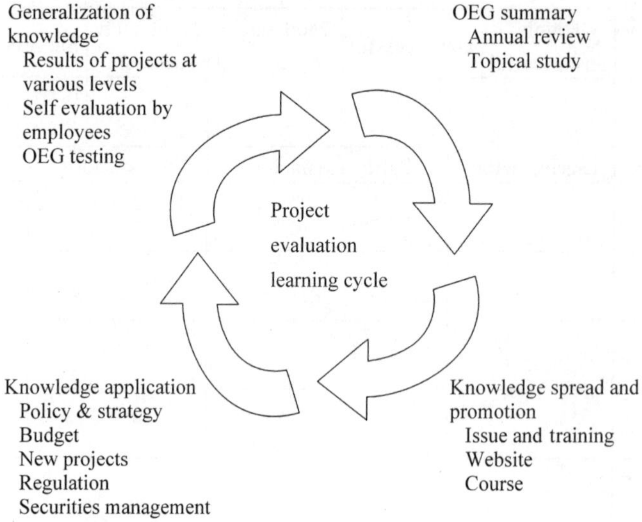

Figure 9.8 Project evaluation learning cycle of IFC

2. Characteristics of post-evaluation of IFC projects

The IFC post evaluation framework is very simple. It mainly evaluates the impact of projects on the economy of borrowing countries, especially the impact on the development of the private sector, that is, carrying out comprehensive evaluation or comparing the impact of projects on developing countries and the impact on IFC itself to see whether the projects have brought about win-win results. It pays particular attention to learning from experience, generalizing, spreading and applying knowledge, thus forming a unique project evaluation learning cycle.

9.2.4.3 Post project evaluation framework of ADB

The post project evaluation of ADB is also carried out by OED. Different from the World Bank, ADB has developed a post evaluation framework that is made up of three different evaluation entities:

ADB's independent evaluation organization: OED;

Self-evaluation organization: ADB's project performance and management department;

Project owner: project performing organization of borrowing country.

OED functions to coordinate the relations between the other two organizations at different stages of project cycle to ensure the smooth performance of projects and make timely adjustments according to actual circumstances. In carrying out post evaluation, self-evaluation organization and project owner each submits a project summary report after the completion of the project. On this basis, OED produces an audit report concerning project performance and sums up the performance and operation of the project so as to use the experience to direct the making of project proposals, screening, performance and completion of projects or as the basis for developing further cooperative relations with member countries and among different regions.

The post evaluation of ADB projects is known as project performance management system (PPMS), which comprises five components: (1) project (logical) framework; (2) project performance report (PPR); (3) project completion report (PCR); (4) project performance audit report (PPAR), and in a limited number of cases, impact evaluation studies; and (5) borrower monitoring and evaluation (at central, and executing and implementing agency levels).

1. Project framework

The project framework is a general anticipation of project performance. It is a design tool for improving quality at entry. Its use aims to ensure a consequential relationship between inputs, activities, outputs, purpose, and goal to ensure the quality of projects. It requires project applicants to use measurable indicators to explain the output and outcome and the social and development impact as well as external conditions and latent risks in project performance.

2. Project performance report (PPR)

The PPR is a management tool for monitoring implementation progress and for improving project information database so as to get the baseline of project performance indicators and calculate the possibilities of the realization of development goals. The report focuses on analysis of problems deviating from the original designs and seeks corrective methods and ways.

3. Project completion report (PCR)

PCR is prepared for all projects separately 1 – 2 years after completion by the executing agency and ADB. It is part of the project self-evaluation. It makes an assessment of achievements against targets and uses the indicators established in the project framework.

4. Project performance audit report and other evaluations reports

The project performance audit report is completed by OED. As an independent evaluation organization, OED uses all the indicators in the framework to evaluate the performance of projects. These independent audit reports, as random samples, use the performance indicators as standards to classify projects into scales and provide guidance to the operations. Other evaluation reports include special case evaluation and study and country project evaluation. The former analyzes and solves some special problems of industries or developing countries and regions or analyzes and evaluates some pilot policies and aid operations of ADB. They also include the evaluation of the values and impact of operations.

5. Borrower monitoring and evaluation report

The report is completed by loan performance organization. It mainly describes and sums up the process of project performance to provide data for the above reports.

ADB sets great store by feedback of its post evaluation system, which ensures the successful spread of the experiences and lessons and evaluation achievements obtained by ADB so as to apply them to the development aid to other member countries. At the same time, the feedback system also enhances transparency of stakeholders of ADB, thus ensuring that aid grants would flow incessantly from developed countries into less-developed countries. The evaluation system and feedback process of ADB are shown in Fig. 9.9.

The ADB evaluation system and feedback process show that such system should be, to a certain extent, regarded as a control and management system, which directly controls and manages project proposal, performance and completion so as to get a timely feedback of the entire process and apply it in directing the performance of future projects. The most important with the system is the project databank, which, by using the technology created by knowledge, constantly replenishes the contents of project framework and performance and management system so as to achieve standard management, thus greatly reducing the repetitive work in evaluation.

9.2.4.4 Post Evaluation Framework of China's Loan Projects

The post evaluation of China's investment projects started in the middle and late periods of the 1980s. In 1988, the State Planning Commission officially entrusted the first post evaluation of a number of key state projects to the China International Project Consulting Co. The earliest post evaluation organizations are the State Planning Commission, the State Audit Office, the People's Construction Bank of

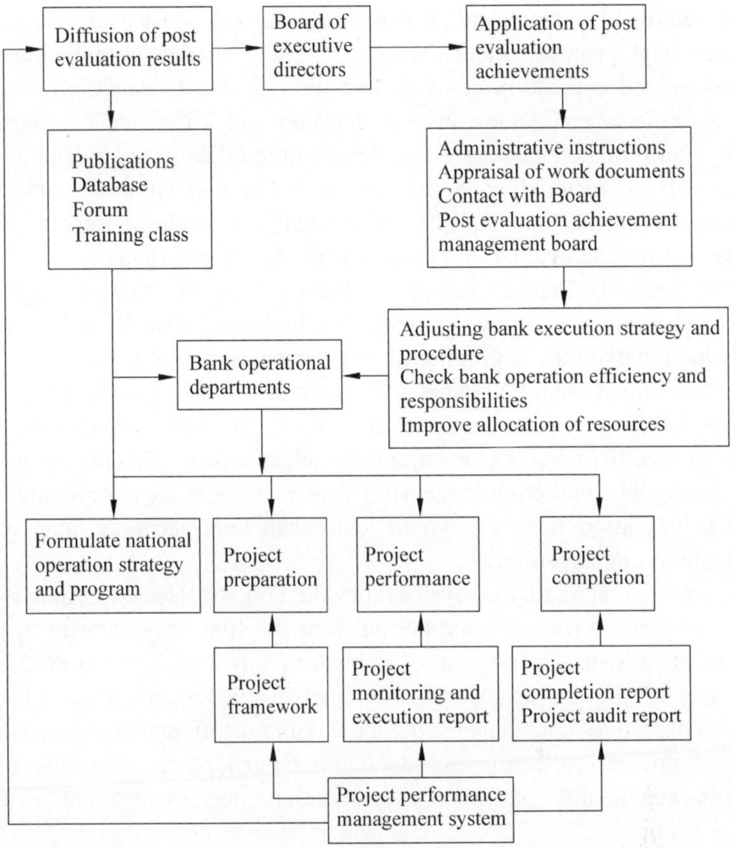

Figure 9.9 Chart of ADB's evaluation system and feedback process

China, the Ministry of Communications, the Ministry of Agriculture and the Ministry of Public Health. In general, the post evaluation of public investment projects is still in the primary stage, far from a standard and institutionalized system. In terms of organizational setup, the organization at the state level responsible for coordinating and directing post evaluation of public investment projects has not been setup. Economic management departments do not have independent specialized post evaluation units. In terms of scope and methodology of evaluation, post evaluation is mainly concentrated on project decision and efficiency of engineering, technology and financial affairs for fixed assets investment projects. Little effort has been devoted to evaluation of the efficiency of the national economy, sustainability and environmental impact. The analysis and evaluation of social impact are still blank. Work on the post evaluation of the allocation of state budget, investment plans and policies have not started yet.

In 1995, the State Development Bank, the China International Project Consulting Co. and the Construction Bank of China started setting up post evaluation organizations, mostly following the World Bank model, and most of them are relatively independent. But most of them do post evaluation of large state investment projects. In evaluating the projects, they mainly borrow the methodology and evaluation contents and the objects of evaluation are mainly individual projects concerning project decision and efficiency of engineering, technology and financial affairs. They devote little effort to the evaluation of the efficiency of the national economy, sustainability and environmental impact. They have not carried out analysis and evaluations of social impact, either. A complete post project evaluation system has not taken into shape.

Up to 1997, the State Development Bank issued the "Methodology for the Analysis and Evaluation of the Quality of Credit Assets of the State Development Bank", which marked the beginning of loan project post evaluation.

The document mainly covers classification of the quality of loans and calculation of item-by-item analysis indicators. The State Development Bank classifies its quality of credit assets into five scales: normal, defective, problematic, serious problematic and credit disposal. Corresponding indicators include rate of overdue loans, deferred repayment of loans, bad loan accounts, loan recovery rate and rate of interest collection.

The credit asset quality analysis and evaluation are carried out in two stages.

The first stage: It covers the period from the first disbursement to the last disbursement of loans. In this stage, the bank mainly analyzes and evaluates the performance of the projects during the loan disbursement period against the anticipated objectives and analyzes the indicators for different scales of loans and the rate of interest collection based on the related plans, statistics, financial documents, statements and project examination, performance and evaluation reports.

The second stage covers the time from the full disbursement of loans to the collection of principal and interests. The analysis and evaluation at this stage mainly cover actual operation of projects after the loans are fully disbursed against the anticipated objectives and the state of the loans and recovery of principal and interests. It calculates according to different categories of loans and the corresponding indicators based on related plans, statistics, financial documents and statements, project examination, performance and evaluation reports and the state of loans and the recovery of principal and interests.

9.2.5 Construction of Indicator and Indicator System

9.2.5.1 Construction of Indicator Systems

The indicator system of project post-evaluation is developed by the logical framework approach (LFA). They are divided into objectives set, process of implementation and impacts after the completion of projects. At the same time, owing to differences in different sectors, the importance of the evaluation results at different levels also varies. This merits full attention in the process of evaluation.

LFA is a designing, planning and evaluating tool developed and used in 1970 by the US International Development Program. The core is to analyze efficiency, results, impact and sustainability of projects from the causal logical relationship of errors.

LFA is a standard method for analyzing the causal relationship and get clear the objectives and inter-related pre-conditions by analyzing associated changes of projects to improve the advantages of designed plan, especially in the planning stage. Numerous practices show that it is a method that gets twice the result with half the effort in constructing an objective logical framework and then plan the project and continue to improve the framework as work is going on, thus enabling projects to go smoothly and making the framework as the basis for supervision and evaluation. The method clearly defines the objectives and the internal and external relations to improve project designs. It builds the objectives of projects at three different levels: macro objectives, direct objectives and output and describes activities, major presumptions, assessment indicators and methods.

LFA emphatically analyzes project objectives and their vertical and horizontal logic of causal relations. Vertical logic refers to input, output and mutual relations of objectives of projects as shown in Fig. 9.10.

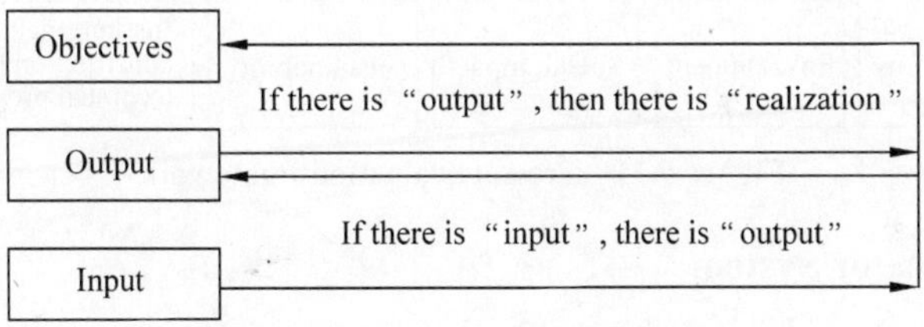

Figure 9.10 Chart of vertical logic

Horizontal logical relationship is made up of originally set objectives, actual results, analysis of reasons and conditions for sustainability. Together with vertical logical relationship, it forms a project post-evaluation logical framework (see Table 9.6).

Table 9.6 Logical framework for project post-evaluation

	Original objectives	Actual results	Analysis of reasons	Conditions of sustainability
Input				
Implementation				
Results of implementation				
Impact				
Project objectives				

By using LFA, it is useful to grasp the causal relations among different factors and approach the problems more systematically and comprehensively, thus avoiding major missing-outs. LFA is designed to find reasons based on results, thus being useful in finding out reasons for successes and failures and in drawing on experience and lessons.

Putting them together and by using vertical and horizontal logics, we may use the following evaluation framework in project post-evaluation (Fig. 9.11).

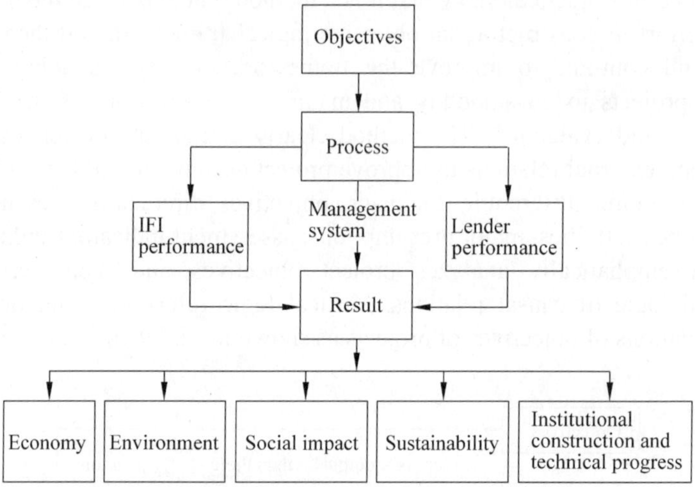

Figure 9.11 Project evaluation framework

9.2.5.2 Indicator System

1. Setting of project objectives

Project objective evaluation is to see whether the objectives sets conform to the actual conditions and study the realization of the objectives. Based on this definition, the objective evaluation may be divided into two levels:

Level one covers the specific objectives of projects, the correctness, rationality and operability of objectives set at the time of project proposal. At the time of project proposal, there might be many reasons that made objectives not very clear or unconformable to market or policy development or too optimistic or too pessimistic of development prospects or major changes took place in the policy or market environment in the process of implementing the projects, thus making the original objectives no longer feasible. This requires the evaluation of the originally set objectives and identification of reasons for the failure of accomplishment and realization. This step is useful to provide experience for the selection of projects in the future and to formulate feasible rules.

Level two covers the evaluation of the realization of project objectives at the time of project completion and during a period of time after completion of the projects. The realization of objectives can be judged from two aspects: one is macro objectives, that is, the general impact and roles of projects on various regions, industries, state economic and social development; the other is direct purposes of projects, that is, to provide products or services or ease supply and demand situation. At this level, the evaluation is to see whether the project objectives have been realized and how they are realized. These manifest themselves in economic efficiency and output and impact on natural environment and social impact.

Our project objective evaluation mainly refers to the evaluation at Level One, with the realization of objectives and their impact evaluated separately in conjunction with the output of projects. In judging particular objectives, we mainly use comparisons to find out changes and analyze the reasons for such changes (Table 9.7).

Table 9.7 Indicators and evaluation grades of objective evaluation

Indicator	HS	S	U
Degree of realization of strategic objectives	Full realization of strategic objectives set after completion of projects	The set strategic objectives basically completed after completion	The set strategic objectives not realized basically or what has been achieved has serious deviated from the set strategic objectives after completion
Degree of realization of direct purposes	The set direct objectives fully realized after completion	Direct objectives set basically realized after completion	Direct objectives set basically not realized or what has been achieved has serious deviated from the set objectives after completion
Rationale of direct purposes of projects	Objectives designed in the project feasibility studies totally tally with the development demand of the project area or totally tally with the requirements of the industry of the project	Objectives designed in the project feasibility studies basically tally with the development demand of the project area or basically tally with the requirements of the industry of the project	Objectives designed in the project feasibility studies not tally with the development demand of the project area or not tally with the requirements of the industry of the project

2. Project implementation

The understanding and grasping of the process of the project implementation are the basis for post-evaluation. Before carrying out post-evaluation of a project, it is necessary to have a comprehensive understanding of the whole process of implementation of the project so as to have a comprehensive grasp of the project and find out where the problems lay, thus finding out solutions and providing policy recommendations and experience and lessons. The project implementation is mainly divided into preliminary policy decision taking stage, project preparation stage, project implementation stage and project operation stage, each stage having its own features and different impacts on the output of project operation.

There are three major factors to determine the operational efficiency of projects.

The first is the project management system. Based on project operation cycle, the management system mainly includes project decision making system, project implementation and management system, fund use and management system and project completion and acceptance system, which exert influence on policy decisions, operations, fund management and output control. In specific operations, these institutional arrangements may be sub-divided in order to find out the procurement and bidding system, fund use and management system, risk control system and completion and acceptance system that have had major impact on the output of projects (Table 9.8).

Table 9.8 Project management system evaluation indicators and grades

	HS	S	U
Institutional arrangements	New institutional arrangements are introduced and play an important role in project operation	New institutional arrangements are introduced and play a certain role in project operation	No new institutional arrangements or institutional arrangements are introduced, but fail to play any roles in project operation
Demonstrative effect	Institutional arrangements introduced play a demonstrative role for similar projects and feature duplicability, and applicability in other projects	Institutional arrangements introduced have certain degree of duplicability and reference value and may serve as a reference for similar projects	Institutional arrangements introduced have sole applicability and cannot serve as a reference for similar projects
Uniformity of operation	Project implementation units and project management units have kept pace from the very start	Project implementing units are consistent, but project management units have altered, or changes have taken place with project implementing units but project management units are consistent	Changes have taken place in both project implementation and management units

Then, the performances of lenders and borrowers also have direct impact on the progress and output of projects. For lenders, evaluation is mainly concentrated on the standards of project screening, project proposal report and feasibility study reports, the supervision over project progress and financial situation in the process of project implementation and their technical support and guidance. For borrowers, evaluation is mainly concentrated on their efforts towards project promotion and publicity, supervision and support, mobilization and participation, as well as writing up summaries and handling post-project affairs after completion of the projects (Tables 9.9 and 9.10).

Table 9.9 Project lender performance evaluation indicators and grading

	HS	S	U
Involvement in project proposal	Involvement of lenders in project proposal advancement, feasibility studies and preliminary evaluation	There is no involvement of lenders in project proposal advancement, but involvement in feasibility studies and preliminary evaluation after projects are approved	There is no involvement in project proposal advancement, feasibility studies and preliminary evaluation or the involvement in these process fails to have a guiding role
Mid-term adjustment	In the process of project operation, lenders direct project implementation units to make effective mid-term adjustment, thus reducing losses of efficiency	In the process of project operation, lenders direct project implementation units to make timely mid-term adjustment and the adjustment failed to achieve better results	In the process of project operation, lenders fail to make effective mid-term adjustment timely according to the operation of projects
Technical assistance and process control	In the process of project operation, lenders send experts to provide guidance to project management and technical progress and carry out effective control of the operations	In the process of project operation, lenders send experts to provide guidance to project management and technical progress, but the guidance is of little importance	In the process of project operation, lenders fail to send experts to provide guidance

3. Project output and impact evaluation

After getting a comprehensive picture of the objectives and process of operation of the projects, we may evaluate their output and results. The evaluation covers economic evaluation, environmental evaluation, social evaluation and sustainability evaluation and evaluation of institutional construction and technical progress.

Table 9.10 Borrower performance evaluation indicators and grading

	HS	S	U
Matching funds	Amount of matching funds and proportion have met the requirements of projects and have been put in place timely	Amount of matching funds and proportion have met the requirements of projects and have not been put in place timely	Amount of matching funds and proportion have not met the requirements of projects
Efforts made	Lenders have done a lot of publicity for project promotion and operation and encouraged local people to get involved and provided guidance to project operations by technical extension and training	Lenders have done a lot of publicity for project promotion and operation and carried out activities for providing guidance to project operations	Lenders have not done any publicity for project promotion and operation or have not paid enough attention to the operation of the projects
Loan repayment mechanism	Lenders have made enough publicity of project loan repayment and established an effective loan repayment mechanism	Lenders have established a certain loan repayment mechanism	Lenders have not established any loan repayment mechanism

Economic evaluation mainly covers project financial affairs evaluation so as to get to know the impact of the projects on the project areas, industries and the state. Focus of evaluation is on the profit-taking ability and loan repayment ability. Key indicators include financial internal return rate (FIRR), net current value and loan repayment period and other indicators for repayment abilities (Table 9.11).

Table 9.11 Project economic efficiency evaluation indicators and grading

Indicator	HS	S	U
FIRR	More than one time higher than benchmark returns	1 – 2 times higher than the benchmark returns	Lower than the benchmark returns
FBCR	More than 2 times higher than benefit-cost	1 – 2 times higher than the benefit-cost	Benefit-cost lower than 1

Environmental impact mainly covers pollution, environmental protection, ecology and natural resources utilization. The evaluation is made to see what ecological effect the projects have and whether or not they can promote sustainable development. In the process of designing and operating the projects, environmental impact may come from two aspects: the direct impact on the environment, such as discharges of waste water, waste gas and solid wastes and the long-term impact, mainly referring to impact on the ecological environment and the minds of the people (Table 9.12).

Table 9.12 Project environmental effect evaluation indicators and grading

Indicator	HS	S	U
Comparable environment indicators	Discharge levels of waste water, waste gas and solid waste can be weakened and noise has totally no impact	Levels of waste water, waste gas and solid waste belong to maintainable intensity and noise impact is weak	Levels of waste water, waste gas and solid waste belong to increasing discharge intensity and noise has certain impact
Comparable ecological indictors	With fairly strong water and soil conservation ability and a stimulating role in biodiversity	With a certain degree of water and soil conservation ability and playing no role in stimulating biodiversity	With poor or totally no ability of water and soil conservation and having unfavorable impact on biodiversity

Social impact mainly refers to tangible and intangible impact on social development and the projects' social motivation and demonstrative effects, which are expressed in the increase in employment and income of local people, in stimulating public policy changes and raising transfer payments of local finances. Evaluation may start from the impact on human capital, on public services and social motivation effect (Table 9.13).

Impact on sustainability refers to objectives sustainability and sustainability of project management and implementation ability and wills as well as sustainability of the overflowing effect. There are many complicated factors influencing sustainability, such as policy changes, management system, financial situation, market situation, technical progress and innovation and culture. This may be evaluated from project continuity, project sustainability and risk control mechanism (Table 9.14).

Table 9.13 Social impact evaluation indicators and grading

Indicator	HS	S	U
Pull to employment	Increasing jobs, basically meeting the percentages set at the time of project proposal	Increasing jobs, covering a certain scope of beneficiaries	Bringing about employment growth to a certain degree but beneficiaries not identical with that in the project proposal

Continued

Indicator	HS	S	U
Changes in the income of participants in projects	Project participants receive corresponding management and technical training and their incomes change significantly	Project participants receive training and their incomes rise markedly as compared with non-project participants	Training is not put in place or income did not change much
Impact on public services	Projects change local government's institutional arrangements and management methods and transfer payments correspondingly	There were no changes in government institutional arrangements, and management or project do not have any impact on local government's transfer payments	Projects do not have any impact on institutional arrangements and management and local government's transfer payments do not change with the projects
Social motivation effect	Projects can attract more private capital to take an active part in the areas and have obvious social motivation effect	Projects can attract private capital and have certain social motivation effect	Project cannot attract private capital and the social demonstrative effect is poor

Table 9.14 Project sustainability impact evaluation indictors and grading

Indicator	HS	S	U
Current operation of projects	After project completion, project implementation units still have the intention to and ability to continue the projects and the project supervision organizations are still there	After project completion, project implementation units still have the intention and ability to continue the projects, but project supervision organizations are dissolved with the completion of projects	After project completion, project implementation units did not have the ability to continue the projects and supervision organizations disappeared
Duplicability of projects	Projects can provide good experience or lessons for similar projects and their management system and ideas are duplicable	Projects can provide certain experience for similar projects but part of the experience has certain special features	Project experience and lessons are independent, unable to be spread for application
Risk dealing mechanism	With good risk dealing mechanism that ensure the continuity of projects after the close of bank accounts	With a certain risk dealing mechanism that ensure a certain financing channels for the operation of projects	Without risk dealing mechanism that cannot ensure project financing after the closure of bank accounts and projects are also closed or delayed

Impact of institutional development and technical progress refers the impact and promotion roles of projects on the utilization of human resources, capital and natural resources of a country or a region, including impact brought about by technical progress and technology diffusion. This is realized mainly by the demonstrative effect of institutional innovation, technical progress and technology diffusion, which have potential and long-term effect (Tables 9.15 and 9.16).

Table 9.15 Technical progress impact evaluation indictors and grading

	HS	S	U
Demonstrative effect	Institutional arrangements introduced with the project have had demonstrative effect and they are duplicable and of reference value and there is already extensive spread	Institutional arrangements introduced with the projects have had a certain duplicability and reference value and may serve as a reference for similar projects	Institutional arrangements introduced with the projects have had only exclusive applicability and cannot serve as a reference for similar projects
Spread of technical training and management experience	Projects have organized proper training and introduced common international practice in project management and have enhanced the management capabilities and experience of related personnel	Projects have organized technical training and introduced some management methods	Technical training have poor results and do not help improve management abilities of related personnel
Spread of project-related research achievements	There are some research achievements and spread of such achievements achieved good results, playing a significant role in production and management	There are some research achievements and result of spread is poor	There are few research achievements and no spread of such achievements at all
Application of information technology	There is special management information system	There is universal application of computers	There are still human and manual management positions and basically no universal application of computers

Table 9.16 Total indicator system

First grade indicators (A)	Second grade indicators (B)	Third grade indicators (C)
Objective evaluation (A1)	Realization of strategic objectives (B1)	C1
	Realization of specific objectives (B2)	C2
Evaluation of implementation process (A2)	Management system (B3)	New system (C3)
		Operation unity (C4)
	Performance of lenders (B4)	Participation in project proposal (C5)
		Mid-term adjustment (C6)
		Technical assistance and process supervision (C7)
	Performance of borrowers (B5)	Matching funds (C8)
		Efforts made (C9)
		Loan repayment mechanism (C10)
Output and impact evaluation (A3)	Economic impact (B6)	Financial Internal benefit rate (C11)
		Financial benefit-cost ratio (C12)
	Environmental impact (B7)	Comparable environmental indicators (C13)
		Comparable ecological indicators (C14)
	Social impact (B8)	Employment pull (C15)
		Changes in income of project participants (C16)
		Impact on public services (C17)
		Social motivation effect (C18)
	Sustainability impact (B9)	Current operation of projects (C19)
		Project duplicability (C20)
		Project risk control mechanism (C21)
	Impact on institutional development and technical progress (B10)	Demonstrative effect (C22)
		Technical training and experience spread (C23)
		Application of project-related research achievements(C24)
		Application of information technology (C25)

The key indicators that weigh the impact and success of projects are different in different sectors and the relative importance of different indicators also varies. For pure competitive projects, economic results and social impact are fairly important, especially financial indicators, sustainability and loan repayment ability; for pure welfare projects, the more important are social impact, institutional construction and technical progress and diffusion. It is necessary to differentiate them in the process of evaluation.

9.3 Evaluation Method Model Affecting the Economic Growth

9.3.1 Growth Effect Evaluation of IFI Loans: Data Source, Variable Construct and Estimation Method

As macro-level research, our data are mainly drawn from various series of China Statistical Yearbook as well as statistical yearbook of related province, *Autonomous Region and Municipality. Series of Yearbook of China's Foreign Economic Relations and Trade*, China foreign economic statistical yearbook and International economic statistical yearbook are also referred to as a important source. Our data cover from 1978 to 2001.

Our data could be categorized into two classes. One is of country-level, including 24 observations. Data used include GDP of each year, growth rate of GDP, growth rate of per capita GDP, total investment, total fiscal income, FDI, taxation, total international trade, export, nominal exchange rate and consumer pricing index.

Other variables which cannot be directly measured are constructed. Where

Efficient labor force—number from historical censors plus newly graduate of each year

Domestic savings—GDP – total consumption

Private investment—total investment – public investment

Public investment—total fiscal expenditure – government consumption

Disposable income—GDP – transfer payment (expenditure for pension and other welfare items by central government)

Import of capital goods—data as machine and equipment import in goods category of international trade

Real exchange rate—average price ratio weighted by trade share of primary trade partners

Growth rate of per capita GDP of trade partners—average growth rate weighted by trade share of primary trade partners

Inflation rate—growth rate of CPI

The second are provincial data, including Guangdong, Hainan, Zhejiang, Jiangsu, Shandong, Hebei, Tianjin, Liaoning, Heilongjiang, Jilin, Shanxi, Henan, Hubei, Anhui, Jiangxi, Guangxi and Yunnan. There are 271 observations in total.

Except efficient labor force, import of capital goods, real exchange rate, nominal exchange rate, growth rate of per capita GDP of trade partners and the like, most provincial variables are similar to the country-level ones. Some specific variables to the provincial model contain population growth rate and ratio of industrial production of non SOE to gross industrial production.

Regarding the new breakthrough in econometrics, we apply three kinds of estimation method with respect to the above data. The first two are applied to the country-level estimation while the third to the provincial model.

First, for single equation model for growth effect and saving effect evaluation, the estimation method, $ARDL(p,q)$ is employed.

Second, for simultaneous equation model, a method developed by Pesaran et al. (1999) is applied. It could be classified into three steps: test for equation efficiency, parameter estimation and model analysis.

Third, specific models for panel data are adopted when provincial data are used to estimate the former models.

9.3.1.1 Econometric Model of Single Equation

Estimation with single equation model is a traditional method in aid evaluation, which was initially introduced in 1960s. This model has been extended mainly in its expressions since early 1990 along with the vast development of econometrics. The general form is

$$\frac{Y\&}{Y} = \alpha_0 + \alpha_1 \frac{A}{Y} + \alpha_2 \frac{S_d}{Y} + \alpha_3 \frac{OF}{Y} + \alpha_4 Z + \varepsilon$$

where

$\frac{Y\&}{Y}$ denotes growth rate of output; $\frac{A}{Y}, \frac{S_d}{Y}, \frac{OF}{Y}$ denotes ratios of aid, domestic saving and other capital to GDP respectively; Z represents various control variables, such as various investment factors and policy variables influencing economic growth. ε denotes perturbation; α_0 is constant.

Table 9.17 gives a single equation model for growth effect estimation.

Table 9.17 Estimation results of single equation model

Variables	Country-level data	Provincial data	East region	Middle region	West region
GY					
Constant	34.22 (3.55)*	10.1 (4.78)*	5.08 (3.04)*	10.68 (4.99)*	6.44 (4.04)*

Continued

Variables	Country-level data	Provincial data	East region	Middle region	West region
D_{east}		− 1.96 (− 2.05)**		− 2.12 (− 2.19)**	
D_{middle}		− 3.18 (− 3.02)*		− 4.06 (− 3.54)*	
GY_{t-1}	0.97 (5.47)*	0.049 (0.96)	0.08 (1.31)	0.044 (0.87)	0.058 (1.13)
IFI_t	− 14.1 (− 2.46)*	− 18.26 (− 4.16)*	− 21.75 (− 4.37)*	− 18.54 (− 4.31)*	− 18.93 (− 4.33)*
$IFI_t \cdot D_T$	19.6 (3.04)*	17.89 (4.11)*	21.49 (− 4.29)*	15.61 (3.56)*	18.12 (4.18)*
H_t	1.01 (3.36)*				
H_{t-1}	− 1.19 (− 4.15)*				
$IFI_t \cdot D_{east}$			− 3.79 (− 1.84)***		
$IFI_t \cdot D_{middle} \cdot D_T$				4.2 (1.96)**	
$IFI_t \cdot D_{west}$					5.25 (1.82)***
SY_t		1.18 (9.69)*	0.13 (3.11)*	1.18 (9.63)*	1.19 (9.94)*
SY_{t-1}	− 0.85 (2.87)**	− 1.14 (− 9.42)*		− 1.13 (− 9.35)*	− 1.11 (− 9.36)*
GX_t		0.03 (2.35)**	0.04 (3.26)*	0.03 (2.37)**	0.025 (2.27)**
N	271	271	271	271	271
LM	5.54	6.17	5.47	6.13	3.64

*Denote the sample based on the 1% statistical result;** Denote the sample based on the 5% statistical result and *** denote the sample based on the 10% statistical result

where

$$D_T = \begin{cases} = 0 & if \quad \text{year} \in 1980\text{s} \\ = 1 & if \quad \text{year} \in 1990\text{s} \end{cases}$$

$$D_{east} = \begin{cases} = 0 & if \quad \text{province} \notin \text{east region of China} \\ = 1 & if \quad \text{province} \in \text{east region of China} \end{cases}$$

$$D_{\text{middle}} = \begin{cases} =0 & if \quad \text{province} \notin \text{middle region of China} \\ =1 & if \quad \text{province} \in \text{middle region of China} \end{cases}$$

$$D_{\text{west}} = \begin{cases} =0 & if \quad \text{province} \notin \text{west region of China} \\ =1 & if \quad \text{province} \in \text{west region of China} \end{cases}$$

GY_t — growth rate of GDP

SY_t — domestic savings

IFI_t — ratio of IFI loans to GDP

H_t — growth rate of human capital

9.3.1.2 Econometric Model of Simultaneous Equation

The estimation method of simultaneous equations has more merits than the previous one and has gotten much newly development in recent decades. It has been extensively applied to evaluation research but not been adopted to systemic country-level evaluation. The leading feature of the method is that it could reflect the endogenous relationship between aid and other explaining variables. That is, it allows for a dynamic interaction relationship. Furthermore, it also has advantages in estimation because it could reduce the multicollinearity, which often occurs in single equation regression.

There are five behavioral equations and two identity equations in our study as following:

Five behavioral equations:

Production growth equation

$$GY_t = f_1(IY_t; GLE_t) \tag{1}$$

Investment equation

$$IGY_t = f_2(GY_t; IPY_t, AY_t, CGY, INF_t) \tag{2}$$

$$IPY_t = f_3(GY_t; IGY_t; FDIY_t, INF_t) \tag{3}$$

International trade equation

$$XY_t = f_4(MKY; YF_t, REER_t, NR_t) \tag{4}$$

$$MKY_t = f_5(IY_t; REER_t) \tag{5}$$

Two identity equations:

$$IY_t = IGY_t + IPY_t \tag{6}$$

$$MY_t = MKY_t + MCY_t \tag{7}$$

where

GY— growth rate of income

IY— ratio of investment to GDP

IGY— ratio of public investment to GDP

IPY— ratio of private investment to GDP

CGY— ratio of public consumption to GDP

XY— ratio of export to GDP

MKY— ratio of capital goods import to GDP

MCY— ratio of consuming goods import to GDP

FDIY— ratio of gross FDI inflow to GDP

AY— ratio of gross IFI loans inflow to GDP

INF — inflation rate or consumer pricing index

GLE — growth rate of efficient labor force

YF — average per capita GDP growth of trading partners weighted by trading share

REER — real exchange rate

NR — nominal exchange rate

Table 9.18 gives a simultaneous equation model for growth effect estimation

Table 9.18 Estimation results of simultaneous equation model

Endogenous variable	Short-term effect of IFO loans	Endogenous variable	Middle-term effect of IFO loans
GY	– 5.89	*GY*	8.39
IPY	– 0.40	*IPY*	14.88
IGY	– 4.23	*IGY*	– 12.67
IY	– 4.63	*IY*	2.20
MKY	– 2.13	*MKY*	0.52
XY	0	*XY*	– 0.11

Where middle-term effect implies the cumulative effect in the sequential five years after the loan flows in.

9.4 Evaluation Model of Substitution Effect

9.4.1 Effect of IFI Loans on Savings

The pioneer studies on the correlation between aid and savings include Griffin (1970), Griffin and Enos (1970). The object of their method, which is among the traditional ones in aid evaluation, is to examine whether aid replaces domestic savings or motivates it.

The general expression of the model is

$$\frac{S}{Y}=\varphi_0+\varphi_1\frac{A}{Y}+\varphi_2\frac{Z}{Y}+\sigma$$

where

S/Y and A/Y respectively denote ratios of savings and aid to GDP. Z/Y denotes the set of influential variables. φ denotes limpacting function of assist on save σ denotes flexibility parameter.

Effect of IFI loans on domestic savings as shown in Table 9.19.

Table 9.19 shows effect of IFI loans on domestic savings.

Table 9.19 Estimation results of effect of IFI loans on savings

Variables \ Region	Entire regions	Individual region
Constant	0.027 (3.24)*	0.03 (3.4)*
D_T	0.013 (3.5)*	0.013 (3.49)*
D_{east}	0.024 (3.39)*	0.02 (2.28)**
D_{middle}	0.014 (2.42)**	0.01 (1.52)
SY_{t-1}	0.86 (35.56)*	0.86 (35.52)*
$GGDP_t$	0.086 (5.26)*	0.086 (5.26)*
IFO_t	2.57 (1.17)	
$IFO_t \cdot D_T$	– 2.78(– 1.24)	– 2.04 (– 1.26)
$IFO_t \cdot D_{east}$		3.05 (1.8)***
$IFO_t \cdot D_{middle}$		1.62 (0.99)
N	286	286

* Denotes the sample based on the 1% statistical result; ** Denotes the sample based on the 5% statistical result and *** denotes the sample based on the 10% statistical result

9.4.2 Effect of IFI Loans on FDI Inflows

How to evaluate the effect of IFI loans on FDI inflows is a new field. The framework emerges from integrated study of three fields. The first is about aid evaluation itself. The second is about the determinants of foreign investment. The third is about relationship of aid and private investment.

The general model form is

$$FDI_t=\varphi_0+\varphi_1 FDI_{t-1}+\sum_{p=1}^{N}\varphi_p\cdot Z_p+\varepsilon$$

where

FDI_{t-1} denotes lag of FDI, Z represents other control variables. Generally speaking, Z includes log of GDP which indicates market size, ration of international trade to GDP which indicates market openness, and log of per capita growth which indicating economic development. φ denotes function, p denotes per capita, ε is perturbation and t denotes time.

In our study, in order to capture the endogenous interactions between all variables, a lag is added to every variable. The modified model has the form as

$$FDI_t = \varphi_0 + \varphi_1 FDI_{t-1} + \varphi_2 \ln GDP_t + \varphi_3 \ln GDP_{t-1} + \varphi_4 \ln PY_t + \varphi_5 \ln PY_{t-1} + \varphi_6 TY_t + \varphi_7 TY_{t-1} + \varphi_8 IFI_t + \varphi_9 IFI_{t-1} + \varepsilon$$

where

FDI_t denotes per capita FDI; $\ln PY_t$ denotes log of per capita GDP; $\ln GDP_t$ denotes log of GDP; IFI_t IFO_t denotes per capita IFI loans; TY_t denotes ratio of international trade to GDP.

Table 9.20 shows the effect of IFI loans on FDI.

Table 9.20 Estimation results of effect of IFI loans on FDI

Region variable	Entire region	East region	Middle region	West region
Constant	285.6 (1.64)	198 (1.22)	157.4 (0.95)	211.72 (1.24)
D_T	40.4 (1.31)	42.34 (1.5)	23.03 (0.79)	31.2 (1.03)
D_{east}	55 (1.71)			
D_{middle}	40.4 (0.47)			
$PFDI_{t-1}$	0.71 (21.17)*	0.65 (16.55)*	0.69 (17.9)*	0.72 (18.66)*
$PIFO_t$	1.86 (3.69)*	0.2 (0.32)	3.6 (5.65)*	1.98 (3.91)*
$PIFO_{t-1}$	1.14 (1.85)***	1.83 (2.1)**	0.92 (1.53)	1.3 (2.1)**
$PIFI_t \cdot D_{east}$		4.58 (4.49)*		
$PIFI_t \cdot D_{middle}$			– 3.92 (– 4.14)*	
$PIFI_t \cdot D_{west}$				– 32.91(– 1.61)
$\ln GDP_{t-1}$	– 22.46 (– 1.88)***	– 14.86 (– 1.36)	– 12.93 (– 1.15)	– 15.9 (– 1.39)
TY_{t-1}		2.54 (6.16)*	2.48 (5.82)*	2.49 (5.71)*
R^2	0.8264	0.8417	0.8626	0.8167
N	264	264	264	264

Where: *PIFO* and *PFDI* imply per capita IFI loans and per capita FDI.

* Denotes the sample based on the 1% statistical result; ** Denotes the sample based on the 5% statistical result and *** denotes the sample based on the 10% statistical result

9.4.3 Fungibility Evaluation of IFI Loans

This kind of evaluation is often focused on examining whether the aid recipient government spends the aid in public consumption or in decreasing taxation. If they do so, the aid capital would not be spent in production and then do little to motivate domestic savings and private investment. This obviously goes astray from the donator's intention.

There are two main approaches to estimating fungibility, one of which we chosen as our basic model is of Pack and Pack (1990, 1993). Because this approach has some drawbacks itself, lack of dynamic structure and macro-wide consideration, and does not allow for some specific features of China's economy, we make some modifications for it. The modified model includes eight equations, among which the former five are stochastic equations and the latter three are equilibrium equations. Those equations have the form as below.

Equations of public sector:

$$CG_t = f_1(T_t, A_t, INF_t)$$
$$IG_t = f_2(T_t, A_t, INF_t)$$
$$T_t = f_3(Y_t, A_t, FDI_t, INF_t)$$

Equations of private sector:

$$IP_t = f_4(IG, YD_t, FDI_t, INF_t)$$
$$CP_t = f_5(Y_{d,t}, INF_t)$$

Identity equations:

$$AD_t = CG_t + IG_t + CP_t + IP_t + NX_t$$
$$YD_t = Y_t + NTR_t$$
$$AD_t = AS_t = Y_t$$

where

CG— Consuming expenditure by government
IG — public investment
T— fiscal income
IP— private investment
CP— private consumption
YD— disposable income
Y— real GDP(gross domestic product)
NTR— net transfer payment
A— gross IFI loans
FDI— foreign direct investment

INF— inflation rate
NX— net export
AD— aggregate demand
AS— aggregate supply
Fungibility evaluation of IFI loans are shown in Tables 9.21 to 9.24.

Table 9.21 Result of Fungibility evaluation of IFI loans

Endogenous variable	Short-term effect of IFO loans	Endogenous variable	Middle-term effect of IFO loans	long-term effect of IFO loans
CG	2.71	*CG*	25.99	50.23
IG	– 3.09	*IG*	– 4.37	– 2.9
T	0	*T*	0.18	– 1.35
IP	0	*IP*	– 0.14	3.13
YD	– 0.42	*YD*	1.09	20.83
Y	– 0.42	*Y*	1.09	20.83

Table 9.22 Result of fungibility evaluation of IFI loans

Endogenous variable	Short-term effect of IFO loans	Endogenous variable	Middle-term effect of IFO loans
CG	0.99	*CG*	3.34
IG	0.03	*IG*	– 0.54
T	– 2.01	*T*	– 6.82
IP	0.44	*IP*	2.04
YD	2.43	*YD*	8.09
Y	2.43	*Y*	8.09

Table 9.23 Result of fungibility evaluation of IFI loans

Endogenous variable	Short-term effect of IFO loans	Endogenous variable	Middle-term effect of IFO loans
CG	0.99	*CG*	3.33
IG	– 0.03	*IG*	– 0.63
T	– 2.93	*T*	– 10.32
IP	0.41	*IP*	1.99
YD	2.28	*YD*	7.87
Y	2.28	*Y*	7.87

Table 9.24 Result of fungibility evaluation of IFI loans

Endogenous variable	Short-term effect of IFO loans	Endogenous variable	Middle-term effect of IFO loans
CG	0.99	*CG*	3.34
IG	– 0.02	*IG*	– 0.28
T	– 1.92	*T*	– 6.61
IP	0.41	*IP*	2.09
YD	2.31	*YD*	8.39
Y	2.31	*Y*	8.39

References

[1] Zhang Sanli. Post-Project Evaluation. Beijing: Tsinghua University Press, 1998. p.1

[2] Austin Hu. speech at the International Forum on the Evaluation of Loan Performances of International Financial Organizations, April 2004